Outstanding Teaching Cases Grounded in Research

Volume 43 • Issue 3 • Summer 2023

Case Research Journal

Published by the

North American Case Research Association

NACRA
NORTH AMERICAN CASE
RESEARCH ASSOCIATION

Editor

Eric Dolansky
Brock University

Published quarterly by North American Case Research Association, Inc.

Cover design, Lisa Fahey, originables.com.

NACRA membership for individuals is US $40. Subscriptions to the Case Research Journal are US $85/year for North American subscriptions and US $115/year for subscriptions sent outside North America.

To join, register and pay online at: https://www.nacra.net/

POSTMASTER: Please send address corrections to:

North American Case Research Association
Christina Tathibana, Assistant Editor
Case Research Journal
crj.christina@gmail.com

Printed in the United States of America

10   9   8   7   6   5   4   3   2   1

ISSN 2328-5095
ISBN: 978-1-7377586-7-9

NACRA Officers 2023–2024

EXECUTIVE COMMITTEE AND BOARD OF DIRECTORS

President

Olga Kandinskaia

Cyprus International Institute of Management

Immediate Past President

Nicole M. Amos

Johnson & Wales University

Vice-President Programs

Melanie Reed

Thompson Rivers University

Vice-President Programs-Elect

Mike Annett

MacEwan University

Vice-President Communications

Atherine Lee

University of Technology, Jamaica

Vice President, Case Marketing

Terry McGovern

University of Wisconsin-Parkside

REPRESENTATIVES OF REGIONAL AND AFFILIATED ORGANIZATIONS

Canada (ASAC)

Meredith Woodwark

Wilfrid Laurier University

Mexico (ALAC)

Martha Elena Moreno Barbosa

Tecnologico de Moterrey Campus Puebla

Eastern U.S. (CASE)

William Naumes

University of New Hampshire (Retired)

Southeastern U.S. (SECRA)

Susan Peters

University of North Carolina

Southwestern U.S. (SWCRA)

Kendra Ingram

Southeastern Oklahoma State University

Society for Case Research (SCR)

Andy Borchers

Lipscomb University

Western U.S. (WCA)

Melanie Reed

Thompson Rivers University

Caribbean Case Researchers Association

Paul Golding

U Technology – Jamaica

International Case Research Association (ICRA)

William Wei

MacEwan University Business School

Directors at Large

Brooke Klassen

University of Saskatchewan

Erin Pleggenkuhle-Miles

University of Nebraska Omaha

Miriam Weisman

Florida International University

Advisory Council Chair

Janis Gogan

Bentley University

Advisory Council Vice Chair

Randall Harris

Texas AM University – Corpus Christi

Case Research Journal Editorial Policy
North American Case Research Association (NACRA)

CASE CONTENT

The *Case Research Journal* (CRJ) publishes outstanding teaching cases drawn from research in real organizations, dealing with important issues in all administration-related disciplines. The CRJ specializes in decision-focused cases based on original primary research – normally interviews with key decision makers in the organization but substantial quotes from legal proceedings and/or congressional testimony are also acceptable. Secondary research (e.g., journalist accounts, high quality website content, etc.) can be used to supplement primary data as needed and appropriate. Exceptional cases that are analytical or descriptive rather than decision-focused will only be considered when a decision focus is not practical and when there is a clear and important gap in the case literature that the case would fill. Cases based entirely on secondary sources will be considered only in unusual circumstances. The Journal also publishes occasional articles concerning case research, case writing or case teaching. Multi-media cases or case supplements will be accepted for review. Contact the journal editor for instructions.

Previously published cases or articles (except those appearing in Proceedings or workshop presentations) are not eligible for consideration. The Journal does not accept fictional works or composite cases synthesized from author experience.

CASE FORMAT

Cases and articles submitted for review should be single- spaced, with 11.5 point Garamond font and 1" margins. Published cases are typically 8-10 pages long (before exhibits), though more concise cases are encouraged and longer cases may be acceptable for complex situations. All cases should be written in the past tense except for quotations that refer to events contemporaneous with the decision focus.

Figures and tables should be embedded in the text and numbered separately. Exhibits should be grouped at the end of the case. Figures, tables, and exhibits should have a number and title as well as a source. Necessary citations of secondary sources (e.g., quotes, data) should be included as endnotes at the end of the case (not at the end of the IM) in APA format. In the IM, necessary citations (e.g., citations of theoretical work from which the analysis draws) should be included using parenthetical author/year embedded in the text (similar to a traditional academic paper) that feeds into a list of references at the end of the IM. Note that the CRJ approaches citations differently in the case and the IM given the differing audiences for which each document is developed (i.e., the case is written for the student while the IM is written for the instructor). In some rare instances, footnotes may be used in the case for short explanations when including these explanations in the body of the text would significantly disrupt the flow of the case, but generally the use of footnotes in the case should be avoided if possible.

The following notice should appear at the bottom of the first page of the manuscript: Review copy for use of the Case Research Journal. Not for reproduction or distribution. Dated (date of submission). Acknowledgements can be included in a first page footnote after the case is accepted for publication, and should mention any prior conference presentation of the case.

It is the author(s)'s responsibility to ensure that they have permission to publish material contained in the case. To verify acceptance of this responsibility, include the following paragraph on a separate page at the beginning of the submission:

In submitting this case to the Case Research Journal for widespread distribution in print and electronic media, I (we) certify that it is original work, based on real events in a real organization. It has not been published and is not under review elsewhere. Copyright holders have given written permission for the use of any material not permitted by the "Fair Use Doctrine." The host organization(s) or individual informant(s) have provided written authorization allowing publication of all information contained in the case that was gathered directly from the organization and/ or individual.

INSTRUCTOR'S MANUAL

Cases must be accompanied by a comprehensive *Instructor's Manual* that includes the following elements:

1. **Case Synopsis**: A brief (three-quarters of a page maximum) synopsis of the case.

2. **Intended Courses:** Identification of the intended course(s) that the case was written for, including the case's position within the course. Please also indicate whether the case was developed for an undergraduate or graduate student audience.

3. **Learning Objectives:** The specific learning objectives that the case was designed to achieve. For more details on learning objectives, see the article titled "Writing Effective Learning Objectives" at the useful articles link.

4. **Research Methods:** A Research Methods section that discloses the research basis for gathering the case information, including any relationship between case authors and the organization, or how access to case data was obtained. Include a description of any disguises imposed and their extent. Authors should disclose the relationship between this case and any other cases or articles published about this organization by these authors without revealing the author's identity during the review process. If the case has been test taught and this has influenced the development of the case, this should be noted. This section should also indicate who in the organization has reviewed the case for content and presentation and has authorized the authors to publish it (note that this last component is not necessary for cases based on congressional or legal testimonies).

5. **Theoretical Linkages:** In this section please provide a brief overview of the theoretical concepts and frameworks that will ground the analysis/discussion of the case situation in theory and research. Please include associated readings or theoretical material that instructors might assign to students or draw on to relate the case to their field or to the course. In developing this section, recognize that business courses are often taught by adjunct faculty who are business professionals who may not be steeped in the theory of the discipline the way an active researcher might be. Develop this section with the intent of helping that type of instructor effectively apply and teach these theories/frameworks.

6. **Suggested Teaching Approaches:** Suggested teaching approaches or a teaching plan, including the expected flow of discussion with an accompanying board plan. Include a description of any role plays, debates, use of audiovisuals or in-class handouts, youtube videos, etc. that might be used to enhance the teaching of the case. Authors are strongly encouraged to classroom test a case before submission so that experience in teaching the case can be discussed in the *IM*. Authors are discouraged from including websites as integral resources for the teaching plan because websites are not static and the content of the website link may change between the writing of the case and an instructor's subsequent use of the case. This should also include a section on how best to teach the case online / remotely.

7. **Discussion Questions:** A set of assignment/discussion questions (typically three to ten depending on discipline) that can be provided to students to organize and guide their preparation of the case. For most cases, either the final or the penultimate question will ask students for their recommendation on the overarching decision facing the decision maker in the case along with their rationale for that recommendation.

8. **Analysis & Responses to Discussion Questions:** This section of the IM represents the core of the case analysis. Repeat each assignment/discussion question, and then present a full analysis of that question that demonstrates application of relevant theory to the case. Note that the analysis in this section should go beyond what a good student might present as an 'answer' to the question. Write to the instructor with an eye toward helping him or her understand in detail how the theory applies to the case scenario, how discussion of this particular question might be approached with students, where the limitations in the theory might be relative to the case scenario, and how the analysis contributes to the building of an integrated recommendation regarding the decision the case protagonist must make.

9. **Epilogue:** If appropriate, an epilogue or follow-up information about the decision actually made and the outcomes that were realized as a result of the decision made.

10. **References**: Provide full citations (in APA format) for all references that were cited in the Instructor's Manual.

REVIEW PROCESS

All manuscripts (both the case and the instructor's manual) are double-blind refereed by Editorial Board members and ad hoc reviewers in the appropriate discipline. Most submissions require at least one round of revision before acceptance and it is common for accepted cases to go through two or more rounds of revisions. The target time frame from submission to author feedback for each version is 60 days.

DISTRIBUTION OF PUBLISHED CASES

The right to reproduce a case in a commercially available textbook, or instructor-created course pack, is reserved to NACRA and the authors, who share copyright for these purposes. After publication, CRJ cases are distributed through NACRA's distribution partners according to non-exclusive contracts. NACRA charges royalty fees for these publication rights and case adoptions in order to fund its operations including publication of the *Case Research Journal*. Royalties paid are split 50/50 between NACRA and member authors.

MANUSCRIPT SUBMISSION

Submit the case manuscript and Instructor's Manual in one document via the *Case Research Journal* ScholarOne website at http://mc.manuscriptcentral.com/nacra-crj. This site provides step by step instructions for uploading your case. You will also be provided the opportunity to upload two case supplements – this is to allow submission of a spreadsheet supplement for the student and for the instructor if needed. No identification of authors or their institutions should appear on either the main case/IM document or on the spreadsheets. All identifying information should be removed from the file properties before submission. If you have audiovisual content to your case, please contact the editor to determine the best way to make this content available to reviewers without revealing the authors' identities.

At least one author must be a member of the North American Case Research Association. Membership dues are included in annual registration for the NACRA conference, or may be paid separately through the main NACRA website.

For questions, contact:
Eric Dolansky, Editor
edolansky@brocku.ca

Adopting *Case Research Journal* Cases
for use in your classes

Faculty members can adopt cases for use in their classrooms and gain access to Instructor's Manual through one of NACRA's distribution partners.

NACRA currently has agreements with the following distributors.

- **Harvard Business School Press** (http://hbsp.harvard.edu/)
- **Ivey Publishing** (https://www.iveycases.com/)
- **The Case Centre** (http://www.thecasecentre.org/educators/)
- **Pearson Collections** (https://www.pearsonhighered.com/collections/educator-features.html)
- **McGraw Hill Create** (http://create.mcgraw-hill.com/createonline/index.html)
- **Study.net** (www.study.net)
- **CCMP [Centrale de Cas et de Médias Pédagogiques]** (http://www.ccmp.fr)
- **XanEdu** (https://www.xanedu.com/)

If you want to use one of these distributors, but cannot find the CRJ case you want, contact the NACRA VP Case Marketing, Terry McGovern, mcgovert@uwp.edu, to see if we can have it added for you.

Textbook authors can also adopt CRJ cases for inclusion in their textbooks for a modest fixed royalty fee. Please contact the NACRA VP of Case Marketing for more information.

From the Editor

As you likely already know, Case Research Journal is the journal of the North American Case Research Association (NACRA). Being a part of this organization has many benefits for the editorial team, authors, and reviewers of CRJ, a substantial one being the annual NACRA conference. The timing of this issue is very close to the 2023 NACRA meeting, held in San Antonio, Texas in October.

For many case researchers, there exists a natural progression for our work, especially if publication in a journal like CRJ is a goal. We bring our cases to a regional conference, which exist all over North America as well as in other parts of the world, receive feedback, and submit that case to NACRA. Using the comments, guidance, and advice we receive at the NACRA conference, we prepare our cases for submission to publishers and journals. This was how my case research and publication journey began; I had a case, sent it to the Administrative Sciences Association of Canada (ASAC) conference, and with the encouragement of mentors there, sent it to my first NACRA conference. The following year, that same case became my first CRJ publication.

Conferences are front-of-mind for me this year because, as part of my duties as editor, I have had the pleasure and honour of visiting many regional conferences. Though I had participated in virtual conferences held by ASAC and the Asociacion Latinoamericana de Casos (ALAC) in 2022, this year I went to the conferences of the Southeastern Case Research Association (SECRA), the Society for Case Research (SCR), and the CASE Association. During the rest of my term as editor I hope to find opportunities to join the Southwestern Case Research Association (SWCRA), Western Casewriter's Association (WCA), the Caribbean Case Researchers Association (CCRA), and the International Case Research Association (ICRA). These regional associations are invaluable for case researchers at all experience levels.

The NACRA conference itself is three days with a community of engaged, knowledgeable, and motivated case researchers, focusing on writing, teaching, innovating, and exploring cases. If you have not attended a NACRA conference, know that it is a different experience from most academic conferences, in that the conversations are mostly focused on collaboration, development, and community, and less on adding a line to an academic resume or poking holes in one another's research. The goal of the conference is for everyone's work and skills to improve, which requires preparation (conference attendees are expected to read and provide feedback on all cases at their roundtable), listening, engagement, and an open mind.

Of the cases in this issue of CRJ, three were previously presented at a NACRA conference: "Tweets, Talk, and Testimony: is Twitter a Publisher, Platform, Public Space, or Something Else?" by Janet L. Rovenpor and Grishma Shah, which takes a topic much in the news, Twitter, and provides a different perspective on the challenges it faces in terms of regulation and ethics; "Caged or Cage-Free?" by Karen E. Boroff, Karen Meleta, and Paula Becker Alexander, a case that takes a different difficult issue, the treatment of animals, and examines a business decision that may be more complex than it initially seems; and "Dr. Wehrheim Winery: To Grow or Not to Grow?" by Marc Dressler and Ram Subramanian, in which two generations of a family-run winery have different conceptions of how to grow. I am confident that if you asked the authors of these cases whether attending NACRA improved their cases prior to submission to the journal, they would say yes.

The other three cases, though not initially discussed at a conference, are no less interesting or impressive. "Columbia Green Technologies (A): Scaling in the Green Roof Market," by Charla Mathwick, approaches quantitative analysis in a case in a very accessible way, and as a result presents a decision-making process that is grounded in data but not overwhelming. "Can Hens Save Dodiya Farms?" by Kinjal Jethwani and Kumar Ramchandani, also involves a fair amount of financial and quantitative analysis, but balances this with qualitative considerations, as the owner of a farm in India makes a diversification decision. "iCreate's Turnaround Proposal," by Andrea Sutherland, Paul Golding, and Lisa Facey-Shaw, takes a look at an attempt by the founder of a Jamaican training company to raise money for a strategic shift; both the financial and governance aspects provide valuable learning opportunities.

In this space I often urge readers of this journal to consider adopting these cases in your courses and urging your colleagues to do the same. Building on the information about the NACRA conference above, another benefit I have found in attending the conference and being a part of a community of case researchers is the access to, and information about, what these researchers are working on. Many of the cases in my case course are included because I learned about them through the NACRA conference. In attending a roundtable related to your area of research and teaching, you will have the opportunity to read and discuss several cases that may end up in your classrooms. So yes, please share the information about the cases in this (and other) issues of CRJ, but also look for other opportunities, such as regional and national (and international) conferences, to build your case courses.

As always, if you have questions, comments, or suggestions, feel free to contact me at edolansky@brocku.ca. I am happy to receive your cases through ScholarOne, to discuss your work via e-mail, and to help you with your own journey as case researchers, with the goal of publishing your work. And if you do come to a conference, and I am there, please say hi!

Sincerely
Eric Dolansky, Editor
Case Research Journal

Contents

COMMUNICATION

Tweets, Talk and Testimony: Is Twitter a Publisher, Platform, Public Space, or Something Else?

Janet L. Rovenpor* and Grishma Shah, Manhattan College [4513 Manhattan College Parkway, Riverdale, New York 10471-4004, janet.rovenpor@manhattan.edu.]

In January 2021, Twitter CEO Jack Dorsey knew he would be asked to testify before Congress about Twitter's role in propagating false news and misinformation. Dorsey described Twitter as a "digital public square" and was a vocal supporter of the U.S. Constitution's first amendment (which protected freedom of speech). Central to his testimony was a controversy involving Internet neutrality: Was the Twitter social media service a neutral platform? If so, each user was responsible for his or her content; Twitter could not be held accountable for slanderous, hateful, or untrue information that users propagated. Was Twitter a publisher? If so, Twitter, akin to news organizations, was responsible for content it propagated. Section 230, an amendment to the Communications Decency Act, further complicated matters, permitting platform hosts to restrict offensive content while shielding them from user-generated content liability. Given this ambiguity, how should Dorsey prepare for the next hearing?

CORPORATE GOVERNANCE

iCreate's Turnaround Proposal

Andrea Sutherland,* Paul Golding, and Lisa Facey-Shaw, University of Technology, [237 Old Hope Road, Kingston 6. Jamaica, 876-909-7603, atsutherland@utech.edu.jm]

On May 17, 2022, Tyrone Wilson, Chief Executive Officer (CEO) and President of iCreate Limited, a fledging creative training institute, needed to fundamentally pivot. The company had made losses since its inception in 2018 and had raised equity and borrowed funds to finance its operations. On December 31, 2021, accumulated losses totaled J$122.1 million. The auditors had raised significant doubt on the company's ability to continue as a going concern and some board members were in muted agreement. The prospect of Wilson losing control of the company, or worse, liquidation, loomed large.

In response, Wilson proposed a turnaround strategy in which a rights issue would be offered to shareholders to raise additional funds. The proceeds would be used to acquire an outdoor advertising company to improve iCreate's bottom line. The plan also included restructuring the company into five divisions: Training, Advertising, Media & Entertainment, Tech & E-Commerce, and Real Estate. He estimated that he could raise J$275 million and the proceeds would be used for inter alia acquisition of a digital advertising company and repayment of debt.

Wilson wondered how the board would receive the rights issue. Were the projections too optimistic? The board meeting was scheduled for May 19, 2022, at 8:00am, two days away; he had little time to prepare to be persuasive and fine tune the details. He made a mental note that convincing the board would be the first hurdle. He would next need to convince the shareholders to subscribe to the rights issue. Based on the previous losses, would they?

CORPORATE SOCIAL RESPONSIBILITY

Caged or Cage-Free? 39

Karen E. Boroff,* Karen Meleta, and Paula Becker Alexander, Seton Hall University [400 South Orange Avenue, South Orange, NJ 07079-2697, karen.boroff@shu.edu]

When Mel Mathers, the chief sustainability officer of a food cooperative, the Independent Food Retailers Consortium (IFRC), was flooded in October 2019 with emails from animal rights activists demanding the cooperative sell only cage-free eggs and make a pledge now to do so by 2025, he had to prepare a brief and recommendation to IFRC's board. In turn, IFRC's board of directors would make a decision on whether to pledge to sell only cage-free eggs in its grocery stores or continue to offer its customers a choice among the different egg production systems. Mathers examined the organization's policy statements, including one on animal welfare. He studied IFRC's financial materiality chart. Mathers began researching egg production systems. Mathers wondered how he could navigate the seemingly contradictory tradeoffs with IFRC's policies, animal husbandry science, environmental impacts, and responsiveness to the many stakeholders in its operating environment.

FINANCE

Can Hens Save Dodiya Farms?   55

Kinjal Jethwani and Kumar Ramchandani,* L.J. University, [Near Sarkhej-Sanand Circle, Off S.G. Road, Ahmedabad, Gujarat, India, 382210, +919898167171 kumarramchandani@ljku.edu.in]

In May 2021 Ranjit Dodiya was seeking a reliable second income stream; he considered whether to launch an egg-laying business. Was this a good idea? How much time would it take to recoup his initial investment? What if sales were not as high as he hoped? What if chicken feed or other operating costs were higher than planned? If he took out loans, would the business be sufficiently profitable to service them? How likely was it that he would be able to set aside some profits from this business to insure against future floods, droughts, and other crop calamities?

The case gives students an opportunity to analyze a current agribusiness operation and a proposed new operation (a Go/No-Go decision). Based on financial and operational analysis, including consideration of foreseeable adverse events that threatened crops, and other foreseeable adverse events that threatened egg-laying, how attractive was this proposition?

STRATEGIC MANAGEMENT

Columbia Green Technologies (A): Scaling in the Green Roof Market   65

Charla Mathwick* Portland State University, [P.O. Box 751, Portland, Oregon, 97207-0751, mathwickc@pdx.edu]

Vanessa Keitges stepped into the role of CEO at Columbia Green Technologies (CGT) in 2010, growing it to become the dominant green infrastructure and green roofing materials supplier on the West Coast. The Portland, Oregon-based company offered customizable green roofing systems that harnessed nature-based technologies to mitigate the damage caused by stormwater runoff. With 2500 roof garden installations under her belt, Keitges wanted to scale her sales and marketing operation to capture the emerging opportunity across the North American market. The green roofing industry was projected to experience a CAGR of 16.2%, building to a $5.37 billion global opportunity by 2030. Working with her executive team, Keitges was preparing for a Q1, 2023 Series C funding round to finance the major rollout of her business. The immediate question was where to locate CGT's expanded sales force and how to prioritize the targeted geographic markets. Compelling business rationale as well as opportunity framing to mitigate the known gender bias in VC funding would need to be reflected in the eventual funding pitch.

STRATEGIC MANAGEMENT

Dr. Wehrheim Winery: To Grow or Not to Grow?   85

Marc Dressler*, Ludwigshafen University of Business and Society and Ram Subramanian, Stetson University [Ernst-Boehe Str. 4, D-67059 Ludwigshafen, marc.dressler@hwg-lu.de]

Dr. Wehrheim Winery, a family business located in the Palatinate region of Germany, faced a critical decision. While the business was controlled by the third-generation owner, Karl-Heinz, his son, Franz, had come up with a plan of launching a secondary line of wines exclusively for the retail channel. Because of the winery's limited supply of grapes from its vineyard, Franz wanted to source grapes from the market for the proposed new line. While Karl-Heinz was reluctant to support the idea because of the risks involved, Franz saw this as the opportunity to showcase his leadership skills as a prelude to becoming the fourth-generation owner of the business. Franz had a month to come up with a sound rationale to get his father's support for the secondary line.

Tweets, Talk and Testimony: Is Twitter a Publisher, Platform, Public Space, or Something Else?

Janet L. Rovenpor, Manhattan College
Grishma Shah, Manhattan College

On January 21, 2021, recently-elected Joe Biden was inaugurated as the 46th President of the United States, despite a violent January 6 attack on the Capitol Hill complex in Washington, DC, by individuals who believed false claims of election fraud.[1] As social media platforms had been noteworthy as places for political discourse during the election and its aftermath, it was widely expected that Twitter CEO Jack Dorsey, among other industry leaders, would be called to testify in an upcoming congressional hearing scheduled for March 25.

In previous congressional hearings, Dorsey and other social media executives were questioned about their views on Section 230 of the Communications Decency Act, which distinguished between neutral web-based platforms (allowed to delete offensive or false content, but not required to do so), versus publishers (legally accountable for falsehoods and some types of offensive materials). While Dorsey long contended that Twitter was a neutral platform whose goal was to enable public self-expression and conversation,[2] months after the 2020 U.S. Presidential elections, 53% of Twitter users believed that inaccurate or misleading information was a major problem on the site.[3]

In a November 17, 2020 online hearing, Senate Judiciary Committee members asked Dorsey about several topics: how Twitter dealt with false claims about the 2020 presidential election process; how Twitter employees determined whether bots or real customers spread falsehoods; whether Twitter monitored Republicans more than Democrats; and other concerns. Dorsey's answers described policies and practices that Twitter introduced before the November 2020 presidential election to prevent bad actors from posting false public service advertisements that urged citizens to vote via Twitter or text messages (**Exhibit 1**), and other dirty tricks based on false information. Among other things, Dorsey said that from October 27 to November 11, 2020, Twitter labeled more than 300,000 election-related tweets as "untrue."

In preparing opening statements for a public hearing, experts advised speakers to state no more than three main points, and to bring along well-organized materials (e.g. PowerPoint charts, important data, etc.) to help speakers reinforce their main points during questioning (**Exhibit 2**). Before the next hearing, Dorsey, who recently stated Twitter intended for users to engage in "healthy conversations," had an opportunity to change his message or keep it the same as in the previous hearings. Was it time for the company to respond more forcefully to misinformation that jeopardized election integrity, public health, or other types of false and potentially harmful tweets?. Given his company's mission and strategic goals, what main messages should Dorsey emphasize?

FAKE NEWS

Until the final few decades of the 20th century, misinformation was spread via word of mouth, mail, printed media, radio, and television. In the mid-1990's, misinformation could also be spread on online networks such as America Online (AOL). A famous case involved Ken Zeran, owner of a real estate magazine, who received harassing phone calls when an Internet troll posted an ad with his username which poked fun at the Oklahoma City bombing.[4] By the 2000s, misinformation spread even more rapidly and broadly via social media and smart phones. The term, "fake news," – "a fabricated story or article, propagated in the same fashion and via the same mediums as real news"[5] – became a permanent part of public discourse when President-Elect Donald Trump refused to allow a CNN reporter to ask a question at a press conference in 2017. According to Trump, CNN published "fake news."[6]

Below are a few examples of misinformation that appeared on social media:

- October 2012: During Hurricane Sandy, a Twitter user falsely reported (among other things) that the New York Stock Exchange trading floor was flooded under 3 feet of water and all electrical power in New York City was about to be shut off.[7] Because statements like these caused panic, the Federal Emergency Management Authority worked hard to correct the false tweets when they were spotted.

- April 2013: A dishonest Twitter user solicited donations for a child, who the user falsely claimed was killed while running in the Boston Marathon in honor of Sandy Hook school massacre victims (a real tragedy in which 20 children and 6 staff members were killed).

- April 2018: Rumors on Facebook, including one that the beating of a truck driver in Sri Lanka (which resulted in his death) was part of a Muslim plot to eradicate the country's Buddhist majority, caused a Buddhist mob to set fire to Muslim-owned shops and homes.[8]

Some users of social media created bogus accounts (using photos and names stolen from real users) and posted fake stories directly. Some users posted sensational headlines along with links to fake news websites. Fraudsters hoped users would click on ads posted on these sites (each visitor click generated advertising revenue for the ad host).[9] Twitter, and other social media sites, had processes to verify a user's identity, especially when the real or supposed user was well-known. Nonetheless, problems persisted. When, for example, Twitter removed conspiracy theorists from its site, many just joined fringe websites (making it even harder to track, monitor, and penalize them).

Sometimes, fake news on social media resulted in the posting of further violent content, hate speech, and harassment.[10] Videos on YouTube falsely accused Maatje Benassi, a U.S. Army reservist, of introducing COVID-19 into the United States just because she had competed as a cyclist in the Military World Games in Wuhan, China in 2019. Her home address was posted online, she received hate messages in her social media inbox, and was the target of death threats.

A *Forbes* story estimated that fake news was responsible for $39 billion in annual losses in the stock market, $9 billion in annual health care costs (due to misinformation about vaccine-preventable diseases), and $9.5 billion in costs incurred to counteract misinformation and repair a damaged personal or corporate reputation.[11]

TWITTER BACKGROUND

Twitter, founded in 2006 by Jack Dorsey, Evan Williams, Noah Glass and Isaac "Biz" Stone, was "a global platform for public self-expression and conversation in real time"[12] (**Exhibit 3**). Twitter users could read breaking news stories, view live-streaming sports events, peruse information that interested them, and connect with other Twitter users who shared similar interests. Jack Dorsey served twice as Twitter CEO. The first holder of that position, he stepped down in October 2008, and became CEO again in summer 2015.

In between Dorsey's stints as CEO, users generated more than one billion tweets per month in 2010, and one billion tweets per week in 2011. Twitter's November 2013 initial public offering raised $1.8 billion. In 2015, the company had not yet turned a profit, its user base was flat, and its share price dropped.[13]

In 2018, Twitter earned a profit of $1.2 billion. In 2019, Twitter, with about 4900 employees, generated nearly a $1.5 billion profit.[14]

Twitter revenues came from two main sources: advertising services (e.g. in 2020, a Starbucks UK tweet introduced its *Truffle Deluxe* coffee flavor) and data licensing (e.g. in 2015, Bloomberg signed an agreement with Twitter that made it possible for financial professionals to track tweet volumes and sentiments).

Dorsey was considered an interesting business leader in the technology industry. He was characterized as having an "oracular beard," and was "something of a cult figure" in Silicon Valley because of his meditation and wellness routines.[15] He was a believer in crypto-currency.[16] At the same time that he was CEO of Twitter, he was also co-founder and CEO of Square, a financial firm. Dorsey's dual CEO roles, as well as his stated intention to live in Africa for a few months, did not sit well with hedge fund manager Paul Singer of Elliot Management, who, in 2020, wanted Dorsey removed as chief executive.[17]

PLATFORM OR PUBLISHER?

Dorsey long contended that Twitter was not a publisher;[18] he and his co-founders never intended to curate content that users posted on it. In contrast, editors at news publishers like *The New York Times* and the *Wall Street Journal* double-checked stories for legal and ethical issues.[19] *The New York Times* mission stated: "We seek the truth and help people understand the world."[20] *The Wall Street Journal* was "the definitive source of news and information through the lens of business, finance, economics and money, and global forces that shape the world and are key to understanding it."[21] Journalism schools trained students to diligently verify source credibility and double-check facts. In contrast, Twitter's co-founders repeatedly stated that users were responsible for content they posted.

From a legal perspective, the distinction between platform and publisher was not clear-cut. The Communications Decency Act (CDA) of 1996 was passed in the wake of public outrage over revelations that some Internet platforms distributed child pornography. In 1997, the U.S. Supreme Court, in *Reno v. American Civil Liberties Union*, ruled that the CDA violated the First Amendment (which protected free speech) because it was too broad, and the Fifth Amendment (which provided the right to a fair trial and protection against self-incrimination) because it was too vague.[22] A subsequent bipartisan effort (led by Republican Chris Cox and Democrat Ron Wyden) modified the CDA. Section 230 of the CDA now stated: "No provider or user of an interactive computer service shall be treated as the publisher or speaker of any information provided by another information content provider" (**Exhibit 6**). Section 230 also specified that a platform provider could not be sued if it restricted access to content "that the provider or user considers … obscene, lewd, lascivious, filthy, excessively violent, harassing, or otherwise objectionable, whether or not such material is constitutionally protected."

Thus, Section 230 both enabled free speech and allowed hosts of digital platforms to moderate content as they deemed necessary, and protected social media companies from lawsuits.[23] A "neutral platform" merely connected users who wanted to converse with one another.[24] Unlike a publisher, a neutral platform could not be held responsible for slander, threats, false information, pornography, or illegal content submitted by its members[25] and was not legally required to monitor user posts or take action on misinformation. If Twitter was classified as a neutral platform, it also could not be sued if it chose to monitor user posts or take action on misinformation. A neutral social media platform could choose to employ content moderators to spot harmful misinformation and it could choose to use automated systems to find, flag, and remove misinformation.

MISINFORMATION DURING THE 2016 PRESIDENTIAL ELECTION

Many pundits were surprised when celebrity businessman Donald Trump won the 2016 election. Trump, a Republican, had never held a local, state, regional, or national political office. His opponent, Hillary Clinton, a Democrat and former First Lady (as wife of President Bill Clinton), served as a U.S. Senator from New York state for eight years, and as Secretary of State in the administration of U.S. President Barack Obama, from 2009 to 2013.

Fake news that propagated via Twitter and other social media convinced some voters to support Trump. In the five months before the November 2016 presidential election, one study collected 30 million tweets containing links to news outlets, from 2.2 million users.[26] Of these tweets, 25% spread fake or extremely biased news.[27] On Facebook, fake election news generated more user engagement than election news published by *the New York Times*, the *Washington Po*st, *NBC News,* and the *Huffington Post* combined, and most of the fake news stories favored Trump or strongly opposed Clinton.[28] False stories contended that Pope Francis had endorsed Trump for President and that Clinton sold weapons to ISIS and other terrorists.[29]

In 2018, Dorsey announced that Twitter would improve its existing processes for verifying the identity and credibility of prominent individuals who had many followers.[30] Russian intelligence agencies had allegedly used Twitter to disseminate fake news, memes, and propaganda via trolls (human users with ill intent) and bots (programs on networks that can interact with systems and users) during the 2016 election campaign,[31] damaging Clinton's credibility and swaying the election in Trump's favor.[32] After investigating, Twitter deleted 50,258 Russian-linked accounts and informed 677,775 Americans that they may have liked, retweeted, or followed fraudulent Russian-sponsored accounts during the campaign.[33]

The Electronic Frontier Foundation (EFF), a nonprofit organization devoted to defending civil liberties in the digital world, aimed to ensure that "technology supports freedom, justice, and innovation for all people of the world."[34] Due to growing concerns about Russian election interference and extremist content, EFF, along with the Northern California branch of the American Civil Liberties Union (ACLU), the Center for Democracy & Technology, and New America's Open Technology Institute, held a May 2018 conference in Washington, DC. Participants drafted the *Santa Clara Principles on Transparency and Accountability in Content Moderation*, which included:[35]

- Companies should publish the number of posts removed and accounts permanently or temporarily suspended, due to violations of their content guidelines.
- Companies should notify each user whose content was taken down or whose account was suspended and describe the reason for removal or suspension.
- Companies should provide a meaningful opportunity for timely appeal of any content removal or account suspension.

On September 5, 2018, Dorsey and Facebook Chief Operating Officer Sheryl Sandberg appeared before the U.S. Senate Select Committee on Intelligence to testify about misinformation and dirty tricks circulated on their social media platforms before the 2016 election.[36] Senators quizzed Dorsey on whether and how Twitter notified users about bot accounts, what responsibility Twitter had to police content, and to what extent Twitter was prepared to deal with computer-generated "deep fake" audio and video clips and other new forms of misinformation that appeared to be authentic. Dorsey replied that Twitter operated as a "digital public square;" and that people around the world gathered to "see what's happening and have a conversation about what they see. In any public space, you will find inspired ideas and you'll find lies and deception,"[37] he said.

Dorsey stated that he did not anticipate the extent to which abuse, harassment, troll armies, propaganda through bots and human coordination, misinformation campaigns, and divisive filter bubbles would travel across Twitter.[38] "We weren't expecting any of this when we created Twitter over 12 years ago," he said. "We acknowledge the real-world negative consequences of what happened, and we take full responsibility to fix it. We can't do this alone, and that's why this conversation is so important, and why I'm here."[39] Dorsey further noted that a "relatively small number of bad faith actors were able to game Twitter to have an outsized impact [on the 2016 election]."[40]

In a November 2018 appearance on *BQ Prime*, Dorsey decried Russia's efforts to suppress voter turnout.[41] One tweet falsely told citizens they could register to vote by sending a text message via an SMS code. Dorsey believed fake news like this was especially problematic when it misled people into doing something ineffective or harmful. He stated that misinformation was a "multi-variable" problem, and that "there's not going to be one fix . . . we are not going to build a perfect solution, it's not possible."

MISINFORMATION IN BETWEEN PRESIDENTIAL ELECTIONS

As campaigning for the U.S. 2020 presidential election heated up in 2019, Democrats accused Republicans of posting fake news, deep fake videos, and other misinformation on Twitter. Dorsey vowed to protect the integrity of U.S. election-related conversations and, later, also to help the public find credible information about COVID-19. At the May 2019 Twitter Annual Shareholders Meeting, Dorsey described three priorities:

- Use machine learning models to detect and remove abusive content.
- Make Twitter easier to use and more conversational.
- Help advertisers launch new products and services.[42]

In June 2019, Dorsey appeared in a TED talk in which he said work continued on Twitter's verification system and that programmers were also developing machine learning algorithms to spot some harassment and harmful misinformation.[43] He added, in hopes of encouraging more thoughtful discourse, that the company was redesigning its site; it would organize tweets by topics, not just by user accounts. "If I were to start the service again, I would not emphasize the follower count as much," he said.[44] He described an MIT study that was testing automated ways to measure "the health of a conversation," along several dimensions. "I want to maximize what people learn from Twitter, not how much time they spend on it," he said.[45] Then, he discussed the difficulties Twitter faced in trying to foster healthy conversations and to reduce uncivil or hateful behavior.

In its 2019 *Censorship Report*, the Electronic Frontier Foundation (EFF) gave Twitter three of six possible gold stars (**Exhibit 4**). Twitter was praised for (a) reporting the number of legal takedown requests it received per country (including type of legal request, compliance rate, number of accounts specified in requests, and number of tweets and accounts ultimately withheld); (b) allowing users to appeal tweet takedowns and account suspensions; and (c) publicly supporting the *Santa Clara Principles*. The report judged Twitter deficient in: (a) reporting takedown requests by country and indicating whether it acted on them; (b) committing to provide notice of tweet removal in cases related to terrorism; (c) reporting on the results of various appeals.

At the May 2020 Annual Shareholders Meeting, Dorsey said Twitter was "working closely with law enforcement, government, and the industry to protect the integrity of U.S. election-related conversations." He added, "We've reintroduced election labels and launched a voting misinformation tool. Our work will continue to increase and evolve until and through election day on November 3."[46] Dorsey said he wanted "to ensure that people can find credible information on our service," by "providing context to what people see, and elevating authoritative content related to the pandemic."[47]

In August 2020, Donald Trump's candidacy was ratified at the Republican National Convention, and former Vice President Joe Biden's candidacy was ratified at the Democratic National Convention. That year, a *Pew Research Center* survey reported that Americans believed fake news was a larger problem than any other issue, such as racism, illegal immigration, climate change, or terrorism (although there was little consensus on which news was fake). 79% of U.S. adults believed that steps should be taken to restrict made-up news, and most Americans believed that government and businesses should work to minimize the confusion caused by it. In contrast, 20% of the survey respondents saw misinformation as protected communication.[48]

In addition to the EFF, other organizations set the record straight on timely topics like the use of masks during COVID-19, voter deception, and climate change. FactCheck – a project of the University of Pennsylvania's Annenberg Public Policy Center – monitored U.S. politicians' statements.[49] On October 20, 2020, FactCheck evaluated conspiracy theories that Trump promoted or shared, including those claiming Biden, and Hillary and Bill Clinton, had committed murders and that mysterious people in the "dark shadows" controlled Biden's presidential campaign.[50] PolitiFact, owned by the nonprofit Poynter Institute for Media Studies, partnered with Facebook and TikTok to flag and rate posted statements' accuracy[51] (**Exhibit 5**).

On October 21, 2020, Ajit Pai, chairman of the Federal Communications Commission, stated that "all three branches of government have expressed serious concern about the prevailing interpretation of Section 230;" an "overly broad" interpretation could "shield social media companies from consumer protection laws in a way that has no basis in the text."[52] In response to Pai's statement, the ACLU urged

Congress to ensure that the Internet remained "a place for self-expression and creation for all."[53] The ACLU asserted that Section 230 protected an "ability to create, communicate, and build community online,"[54] and it warned that holding platforms liable for user-generated content might lead platform hosts to either over-censor, or to choose not to flag misinformation.

On October 28 – one week before the November 3, 2020 U.S. presidential election – Dorsey and other social media CEOs testified before the U.S. Senate Committee on Commerce, Science and Transportation. Republican Senator and Chair Roger Wicker of Mississippi sought to revise Section 230; he said platform hosts had had "the ability to control, stifle, and even censor content in whatever manner meets their respective standards," and that recent incidents showed a "censorship and suppression of conservative voices on the internet."[55] Democratic Senator Ed Markey of Massachusetts expressed concern that social media companies allowed too many dangerous posts to remain up, "amplifying harmful content so that it spreads like wildfire and torches our democracy."[56] Republican Senator Ted Cruz of Texas said, "Twitter's conduct has by far been the most egregious;" he contended that Twitter went too far in silencing people and blocking political speech.

Senator Cruz also noted that Twitter blocked a retweeted *New York Post* story about unsavory content allegedly retrieved from a laptop owned by President Biden's son Hunter. "Mr. Dorsey, who the hell elected you and put you in charge of what the media are allowed to report and what the American people are allowed to hear?" Cruz said. "Why do you persist in behaving as a Democratic super PAC, silencing views contrary to your political beliefs?"[57] In response, Democratic Senator Brian Schatz of Hawaii called the hearing a "sham." He warned CEOs: "don't let the specter of removing Section 230 protections or an amendment to antitrust law, or any other kinds of threats cause you to be a party to the subversion of our democracy."[58] Talking to social media companies, Schatz said, "The truth is, that because some of my colleagues accuse you, your companies, and your employees of being biased or Liberal, you have institutionally bent over backwards and overcompensated. You've hired Republican operatives, hosted private dinners with Republican leaders, and in contravention over your terms of service, given special dispensation to right-wing voices and even throttled progressive journalism."[59]

In response to these concerns, Dorsey stated that Twitter transparently published its policies and practices and answered questions about how content was moderated. He said Twitter's anti-misinformation policy covered media manipulation, public health misinformation (especially regarding COVID-19), and election interference, and that Twitter defined objectionable content as "anything that is limiting … the speech of others."[60] Dorsey said Twitter wanted its users to feel safe on its platform, free from abuse, harassment, and misleading information.

A CONTENTIOUS 2020 PRESIDENTIAL ELECTION

The 2020 presidential election was held Tuesday, November 3. By November 7, it was widely reported that Biden won with more than 51% of the popular vote and likely enough Electoral College votes. Trump won 47% of the popular vote. Claiming election fraud, Trump refused to acknowledge Biden as President-Elect.

On November 17, 2020, Dorsey testified in a hearing of the U.S. Senate Committee on the Judiciary entitled, *Breaking the News: Censorship, Suppression and the 2020 Election.*[61]

Republican Senator Lindsey Graham of South Carolina, chair of the hearing, noted that a 2018 Pew Research Center survey (of nearly 750 13- to 17-year-olds) found that 97% of respondents used social media platforms like YouTube, Facebook, Instagram, and Snapchat. The purpose of the hearing, he said, was to "look at Section 230 to see if it needs to be modified or changed," because it "allows social media platforms like Twitter and Facebook to pass on information without legal liability."[62]

During this hearing, Democratic Senator Richard Blumenthal of Connecticut said that President Trump used Twitter as a microphone "to spread vicious falsehoods . . . every day, he posts new threats and conspiracy theories about mail-in ballots and voting machines, lies that contradict his own election security officials and lawyers."[63] Blumenthal stated that social media leaders had built "terrifying tools of persuasion and manipulation, with power far exceeding the robber barons of the last Gilded Age."[64] He warned: "you have immense civic and moral responsibility to ensure that these instruments of influence do not irreparably harm our country."[65]

Republican senators again asked Dorsey why Twitter prevented a *New York Post* story about photos on Hunter Biden's laptop from being spread (a decision which Twitter reconsidered and corrected within 24 hours). Senator Graham asked how Twitter employees decided which content was reliable or unreliable. Dorsey replied that misinformation was "hard to define;"[66] Twitter's main criterion was to avoid severe harm. Twitter currently focused on manipulated media, election integrity, and public health, he said, adding that Twitter's policies were "living documents" that evolved over time.[67]

In subsequent written testimony, Dorsey indicated that toxic misinformation issues could be resolved if all social media companies would:[68]

a) regularly publish and update content moderation rules that intend to allow individuals to participate in public conversations freely and safely, ensure that the general public understand these rules and policies, and ensure that employees enforce their rules and follow their policies;
b) implement a straightforward process for people to appeal decisions made by social media companies when they believe they are not fair;
c) give people choices about the algorithms used to deliver content to ensure it is most relevant to them.

On December 14, Biden's victory was ratified by the Electoral College. Even so, the Trump campaign team still claimed election fraud. Investigations were conducted in several contested states,[69] but no evidence of fraud sufficient to change the election result was ever identified.

On January 6, 2023, Trump supporters attended a Washington DC rally, then some participated in a violent attack on the U.S. Capitol. On January 7, the presidential election results were certified by Congress. On January 13, University of Texas researcher Sam Woolly stated that during the campaign Trump turned Twitter into a political tool that "spread propaganda and manipulated public opinion," and that Trump used Twitter to "delegitimize the positions of his opponents."[70]

As of January 21, 2021 (the day President Joe Biden was sworn into office), and beyond, Section 230 remained in effect. Jack Dorsey had an opportunity to start preparing for an announced congressional hearing in March (a formal invitation was forthcoming, but the date was not quite settled). "Fake News" continued to propagate on Twitter, despite Dorsey's commitment to "healthy conversations" on its "digital public square." Among others, Dorsey would face three congressmen who had issued a joint statement that "big tech has failed to acknowledge the role they've played in fomenting and elevating blatantly false information to its online audiences. Industry self-regulation has failed."[71]

Thus, it could be seen that Dorsey had a responsibility to review the steps Twitter had taken thus far to curb harmful misinformation. In addition, the debate over whether his company could retain its status as a neutral platform under Section *230* might surface again during the hearing. Dorsey would be advised to reflect on and re-articulate his position on how Twitter can best serve society by allowing free speech and preventing undue harm to others. Perhaps some of Twitter's policies or priorities needed to change. Perhaps some new actions needed to be taken. An approach, supported by expertise, would be that Dorsey and his team would need to prepare a persuasive message with three main points that he could present during his opening remarks. It would be most helpful if Dorsey had some useful notes that he could refer back to during a hearing that could last several long hours.

Exhibit 1 - November 1, 2017, Senate Judiciary Subcommittee on Crime and Terrorism

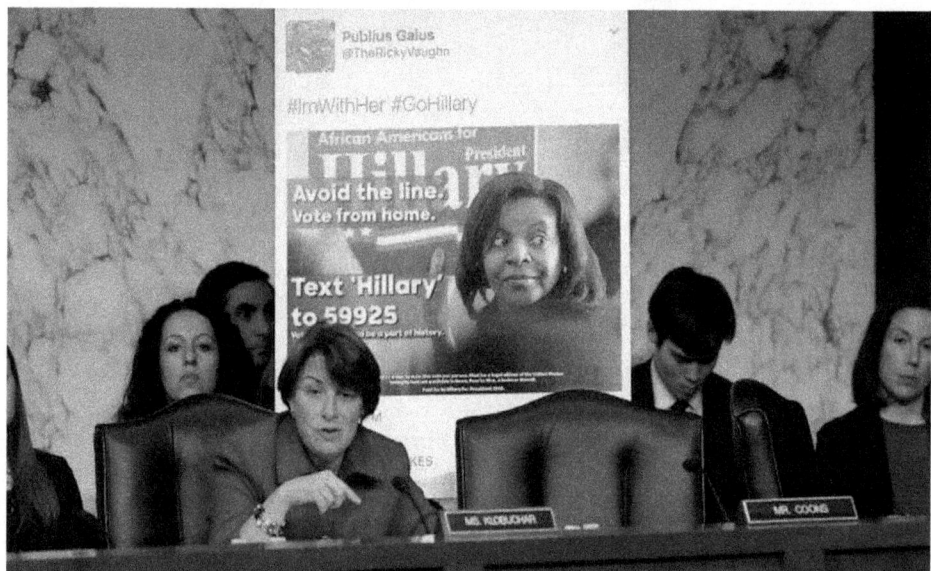

Source: Stewart, E. "Banks have to know their customers. Shouldn't Facebook and Twitter? *Vox*, March 19, 2018. https://www.vox.com/policy-and-politics/2018/3/19/17038130/facebook-twitter-russia-regulations-laws

Exhibit 2 - U.S. Congressional Hearings

The United States Government Publishing Office defines a congressional hearing as "a meeting or session of a Senate, House, joint, or special committee of Congress, usually open to the public, to obtain information and opinions on proposed legislation, conduct an investigation, or evaluate/oversee the activities of a government department or the implementation of a Federal law. In addition, hearings may also be purely exploratory in nature, providing testimony and data about topics of current interest." Source: https://www.govinfo.gov/help/chrg , 18 Jan 2023.

Congress.Gov, the "official website for U.S. federal legislative information, ... provides access to accurate, timely, and complete legislative information for Members of Congress, legislative agencies, and the public. It is presented by the Library of Congress (LOC), using data from the Office of the Clerk of the U.S. House of Representatives, Office of the Secretary of the Senate, the Government Publishing Office, Congressional Budget Office, and the LOC's Congressional Research Service. ... Congress.gov is usually updated the morning after a session adjourns. Consult Coverage Dates for Congress.gov Collections for specific update schedules and start date for each collection". Source: Congress.gov/about, 18 Jan 2023. Congress.Gov defines congressional hearings as follows:

> "Committee hearings are a method by which committee members gather information to inform committee business. Business dealt with by hearings may be broadly classified into four types: legislative, oversight, investigative, and consideration of presidential nominations. The Committee Consideration video tutorial explains hearings within the context of the legislative process. Nomination hearings are explained in the Executive Business in the Senate video tutorial. Hearings may be held on Capitol Hill or elsewhere (e.g. a committee member's district or state, or a site related to the subject of the hearing)."

Sources: https://www.congress.gov/help/committee-materials as of 18 Jan 2023

Committee Consideration video: https://www.congress.gov/legislative-process/committee-consideration

Note: Congress.gov supersedes the THOMAS system which was retired on July 5, 2016.

Various other publications offer guidance about preparing for congressional hearings. For example, on a blog, among *12 Tips for Testifying Before Congress,* five recommendations are:

- Be selective; only testify if you have genuine expertise to offer. ...
- Submit a written statement before testifying [but] deliver a time-limited opening statement of less than five minutes. ...
- Pick three main points to emphasize ...
- Prepare answers to questions you are likely to receive ...
- Keep your answers short ...

Source: Charles Blahous, The Dirty Dozen: 12 Tips for Testifying Before Congress. Manhattan Institute for Policy Research, June 25, 2019. https://economics21.org/12-tips-for-testifying-before-congress,

Exhibit 3 - Key Twitter Events

2004 In November, Evan Williams, Noah Glass, and Biz Stone founded podcaster Odeo. Jack Dorsey became its CEO.
2006 In March, Dorsey sent his first tweet. In July, Noah Glass left Odeo.
2007 Shortly after Twitter was demonstrated at a music and art festival in Texas, Twitter was spun off as an independent company.
2009 In September, users could identify real celebrity accounts via a new system. In October, users could launch an investigation into a questionable user profile by clicking on a "Report as Spam" button.
2010 In June, Twitter promised it would set up a security system to prevent hackers from hijacking accounts of prominent users and sending out misinformation.
2011 In September, Twitter reached 100 million monthly active users.
2012 In December, Twitter passed 200 million monthly active users.
2013 In May, Twitter implemented a new login verification system as a second check to verify a user's identity. In November, Twitter went public and was valued at $31 billion.
2016 In July, all users, not just public figures or celebrities, could apply for a "verified" checkmark badge. In September, Twitter joined First Draft Coalition to fight the spread of fake news. In December, a fake Twitter news story led to a Pakistani-Israeli confrontation.
2017 In June, Twitter tested a feature allowing users to flag tweets containing misinformation. In September and October, Twitter identified almost 3,000 accounts and 36,000 bots linked to Russia which tried to influence the 2016 U.S. Presidential Election. A few months later, the number of accounts rose to 3,814.
2018 In February, Twitter updated its rules to prevent Bot operators with multiple accounts from simultaneously tweeting, liking posts, and following accounts. In November, Twitter expanded from the previous limit of 140 characters per tweet to 280.
2019 In January, Twitter de-activated 764 fake accounts linked to Venezuela. This was in addition to 2,617 fake accounts linked to Iran that had been previously removed. In February, Twitter reported it had 126 million daily active users. In June, Twitter stated that there were thousands of fake accounts linked to foreign governments, including Iran and Russia.

In August, Twitter removed 936 Chinese accounts that attempted to undermine antigovernment protests in Hong Kong.
2020 In March, Twitter removed over 1,100 tweets containing misinformation about COVID-19. In April, Twitter deleted 20,000 fake accounts lined to Saudi, Serbian, and Egyptian governments. In May, Twitter placed a fact-check label on President Trump's tweets for the first time. In June, Twitter removed 174,000 fake accounts operated by the Chinese government. In July, Twitter banned 7,000 QAnon (a widespread consipiracy group) accounts to curb harassment and misinformation. In August, Twitter removed a video of Trump claiming that children were "almost immune" from COVID-19. In October, Twitter suspended fake accounts posing as Black Trump supporters. In November, Twitter applied labels to 300,000 tweets for content that was disputed or misleading.

Sources: Adapted and updated from Meyer, J. "History of Twitter: Jack Dorsey and the social media giant." *Thestreet.com*, June 18, 2019. Retrieved from https://www.thestreet.com/technology/history-of-twitter-facts-what-s-happening-in-2019-14995056; Twitter, Inc. *International Directory of Company Histories*, vol. 189 (2017). JP Pederson (Ed.). Farmington Hills, MI: St. James Press. *Business Insights: Essentials*. Web. 3 Apr. 2021; Scola, N. "Silicon Valley Game-Plans for a Messy Election Night." *Politico*, August 12, 2020. Retrieved from: https://www.politico.com/news/2020/08/12/election-silicon-valley-394354

Exhibit 4 - Electronic Frontier Foundation 2019 *Who Has Your Back*? Report (adapted)

	Legal Requests	Platform Policy Requests	Notice	Appeals Mechanisms	Appeals Transparency	Santa Clara Principles
Facebook			★			★
Instagram						★
LinkedIn				★		★
Pinterest	★	★		★		
Reddit	★	★	★	★	★	★
Snap	★	★				★
Tumblr				★		★
Twitter	★			★		★
YouTube	★	★		★		★

Source: Who Has Your Back? Censorship Edition 2019 https://www.eff.org/wp/who-has-your-back-2019

Exhibit 5 - Examples of Tweets Evaluated by PolitiFact.com

PolitiFact Truth Levels

TRUE   Statement is accurate and nothing significant is missing.

MOSTLY TRUE   Statement is accurate but needs clarification or additional information.

HALF TRUE   Statement is partially accurate but leaves out important details or takes things out of context.

MOSTLY FALSE   Statement contains an element of truth but ignores critical facts that would give a different impression.

FALSE   Statement is not accurate.

PANTS ON FIRE   Statement is not accurate and makes a ridiculous claim.

North Carolina Republican Party

stated on December 27, 2020 in a tweet:

North Carolina Gov. Roy Cooper "has not left the Governor's Mansion since the start of the #COVID19 crisis."

By Paul Specht · December 29, 2020

PANTS ON FIRE!

Marco Rubio

stated on December 27, 2020 in a tweet:

Says "Dr. Fauci lied about masks in March."

By Jon Greenberg · December 28, 2020

FALSE

Christi Craddick

stated on December 12, 2020 in a tweet:

Says that the oil and gas industry comprises 35% of the Texas economy.

By Brandon Mulder · December 22, 2020

MOSTLY TRUE

Exhibit 6 - Excerpts from Section 230 of the Communications Decency Act (CDA)

(a) Findings The Congress finds the following:

(1) The rapidly developing array of Internet and other interactive computer services available to individual Americans represent an extraordinary advance in the availability of educational and informational resources to our citizens.
(2) These services offer users a great degree of control over the information that they receive, as well as the potential for even greater control in the future as technology develops.
(3) The Internet and other interactive computer services offer a forum for a true diversity of political discourse, unique opportunities for cultural development, and myriad avenues for intellectual activity.
(4) The Internet and other interactive computer services have flourished, to the benefit of all Americans, with a minimum of government regulation.
(5) Increasingly Americans are relying on interactive media for a variety of political, educational, cultural, and entertainment services.

(b) Policy It is the policy of the United States –

(1) to promote the continued development of the Internet and other interactive computer services and other interactive media;
(2) to preserve the vibrant and competitive free market that presently exists for the Internet and other interactive computer services, unfettered by Federal or State regulation;
(3) to encourage the development of technologies which maximize user control over what information is received by individuals, families, and schools who use the Internet and other interactive computer services;
(4) to remove disincentives for the development and utilization of blocking and filtering technologies that empower parents to restrict their children's access to objectionable or inappropriate online material; and
(5) to ensure vigorous enforcement of Federal criminal laws to deter and punish trafficking in obscenity, stalking, and harassment by means of computer.

(c) Protection for "Good Samaritan" blocking and screening of offensive material
(1) Treatment of publisher or speaker
No provider or user of an interactive computer service shall be treated as the publisher or speaker of any information provided by another information content provider.
(2) Civil liability
No provider or user of an interactive computer service shall be held liable on account of –
A. any action voluntarily taken in good faith to restrict access to or availability of material that the provider or user considers to be obscene, lewd, lascivious, filthy, excessively violent, harassing, or otherwise objectionable, whether or not such material is constitutionally protected; or

B. any action taken to enable or make available to information content providers or others the technical means to restrict access to material described in paragraph.

Source: 47 U.S. Code 230 – Protection for private blocking and screening of offensive material (https://www.law.cornell.edu/uscode/text/47/230)

NOTES

[1] People participating in the violence thought Biden did not fairly win the November 2020 elections; investigations affirmed Biden's election.

[2] Twitter Fiscal Year 2020 Annual Report. https://investor.twitterinc.com/financial-information/annual-reports/default.aspx

[3] McClain, C., Widjaya, R., Rivero, G., & Smith, A. "The Behavior and Attitudes of U.S. Adults on Twitter," Pew Research Center, November 15, 2021.

[4] Allyn, B. "The Story of Section 230 Goes Back to an AOL Troll. Now the Law May Be Undone." NPR, February 22, 2023. https://www.npr.org/2021/05/11/994395889/how-one-mans-fight-against-an-aol-troll-sealed-the-tech-industrys-power

[5] Vojak, B. "Fake news: The commoditization of Internet speech." California Western International Law Journal, 48 (1), (2017), 123-158. Retrieved from https://scholarlycommons.law.cwsl.edu/cwilj/vol48/iss1/5/

[6] Slack, D. "Trump to CNN: 'You are fake news.'" USA Today, January 11, 2017. Retrieved from https://www.usatoday.com/story/news/politics/onpolitics/2017/01/11/trump-cnn-press-conference/96447880/

[7] Kaczynski, A. "How One Well-Connected Pseudonymous Twitter Spread Fake News about Hurricane Sandy," Buzz Feed Politics, October 30, 2012. Retrieved from https://buzzfeedpolitics.tumblr.com/post/34623254677/how-one-well-connected-pseudonymous-twitter-spread

[8] Taub, A, & Fisher, M. "Where Countries are Tinderboxes and Facebook is a Match." The New York Times, April 21, 2018. https://www.nytimes.com/2018/04/21/world/asia/facebook-sri-lanka-riots.html

[9] "Where does fake news come from?" Retrieved from https://www.cits.ucsb.edu/fake-news/where

[10] Frenkel, S. "Facebook to Remove Misinformation that Leads to Violence," The New York Times, July 18, 2018. https://www.nytimes.com/2018/07/18/technology/facebook-to-remove-misinformation-that-leads-to-violence.html; Frenkel, S., Isaac, M., & Conger, K. "On Instagram, 11,696 Examples of How Hate Thrives on Social Media," The New York Times, October 29, 2018. https://www.nytimes.com/2018/10/29/technology/hate-on-social-media.html

[11] McElhaney, A. "Fake news creates real losses." Institutional Investor, November 18, 2019. Retrieved from

https://www.institutionalinvestor.com/article/b1j2ttw22xf7n6/Fake-News-Creates-Real-Losses

[12] Twitter Fiscal Year 2020 Annual Report. https://investor.twitterinc.com/financial-information/annual-reports/default.aspx

[13] Wilhelm, A., & Lynley, M. "Twitter's fiscal 2015: Up, flat, and down." TechCrunch, December 24, 2015. https://techcrunch.com/2015/12/24/twitters-fiscal-2015-up-flat-and-down/

[14] Twitter Inc.'s 10-K, filed February 18, 2020. From www.sec.gov.

[15] Roose, K. "Dorsey's Twitter departure hints at Tech Moguls' Restlessness." The New York Times, November 30, 2021.

[16] Ibid.

[17] Brown, A. "Twitter's Jack Dorsey Has a New Nemesis: Hedge Gund Billionaire Paul Singer." Forbes, February 29, 2020. https://www.forbes.com/sites/abrambrown/2020/02/29/twitters-jack-dorsey-has-a-new-nemesis-hedge-fund-billionaire-paul-singer/?sh=259fdaa027d8

[18] "Dorsey's Response to Senator Tillis' Questions, Senate Judiciary Committee," IPWatchdog, November 17, 2020. From https://ipwatchdog.com/wp-content/uploads/2020/12/Dorsey-Response-QFRs.pdf; "Mark Zuckerberg & Jack Dorsey Testimony Transcript Senate Tech Hearing November 17," https://www.rev.com/blog/transcripts/mark-zuckerberg-jack-dorsey-testimony-transcript-senate-tech-hearing-november-17 and

[19] Laurenson, L. "Don't try to be a publisher and a platform at the same time," Harvard Business Review, January 19, 2015.

[20] https://www.nytco.com>Company

[21] https://www.nytco.com/company/; https://www.wsj.com/about-us?mod=wsjfooter

[22] "Reno v. ACLU, 521 U. S. 844 (1997)." U.S. Supreme Court. https://supreme.justia.com/cases/federal/us/521/844/

[23] Stemler, A. "What is Section 230? An expert on internet law and regulation explains the legislation that paved the way for Facebook, Google, and Twitter." The Conversation U.S., August 2, 2021.

[24] Chander, A, & Krishnamurthy, V. "The myth of platform neutrality," Georgetown Law Technology Review, 2.2 (2018), 401-416.

[25] An aggrieved party or victim of defamation might have been able to sue an individual user for slander if the user could be found and identified and if a case proving harm could be made in the courts. The social media company could not be sued.

[26] Bovet, A., & Makse, H. A. "Influence of fake news in Twitter during the 2016 U.S. presidential election. Nature Communications, 10 (2019) (7), p. 1. Retrieved from https://www.nature.com/articles/s41467-018-07761-2

[27] Ibid.

28 Silverman, C. "This Analysis Shows how Viral Fake Election News Stories Outperformed Real News on Facebook." BuzzFeed News, November 16, 2016. https://www.buzzfeednews.com/article/craigsilverman/viral-fake-election-news-outperformed-real-news-on-facebook

29 Ibid.

30 Barron, L. "Twitter wants to verify all users as a way to prove identity. Fortune Magazine, March 9, 2018. https://fortune.com/2018/03/09/twitter-verification-all-users/

31 Porter, T. "If you shared one of these tweets during the 2016 election then you were duped by Russian fake news." Newsweek, January 20, 2018. Retrieved from https://www.newsweek.com/if-you-shared-one-these-tweets-during-2016-election-then-you-were-duped-786075

32 A "troll" was a person who intentionally baited others, created a stir, or drew attention to their causes. A "bot" was a piece of software that created content on social media.

33 Porter, T. (2018), op cit.

34 "About EFF." https://www.eff.org/about

35 "The Santa Clara Principles." https://santaclaraprinciples.org

36 Manjoo, Farhad. What Jack Dorsey and Sheryl Sandberg taught Congress and vice versa. The New York Times, Sep. 6, 2018.

37 "Hearing before the Select Committee on Intelligence of the United States Senate, One Hundred Fifteenth Congress, Second Session," U.S. Government Publishing Office, 2019. Retrieved from https://www.govinfo.gov/content/pkg/CHRG-115shrg31350/pdf/CHRG-115shrg31350.pdf

38 "Statement of Jack Dorsey, Chief Executive Officer, Twitter, Inc.," https://www.intelligence.senate.gov/hearings/open-hearing-foreign-influence-operations'-use-social-media-platforms-company-witnesses#

39 Popken, B. "Apologies and promises: Facebook and Twitter tell senators they will do more to combat misinformation. NBCNews, September 5, 2018. Retrieved from https://www.nbcnews.com/tech/tech-news/apologies-promises-facebook-twitter-tell-senators-they-will-do-more-n906731

40 Ibid.

41 "Fake news a multi-variable problem, says Twitter CEO Jack Dorsey." BQ Prime, November 12, 2018. https://www.youtube.com/watch?v=hmHhLjyxD8k

42 "Twitter Inc. Annual Shareholders Meeting-Final." Fair Disclosure Wire, May 20, 2019.

43 Dorsey, Jack, "How Twitter needs to change," TED, June 7, 2019. https://www.youtube.com/watch?v=BcgDvEdGEXg

44 Ibid.

45 Ibid.

46 Twitter Inc. Annual Shareholders Meeting-Final." Fair Disclosure Wire, May 27, 2020.

47 Ibid.

48 Mitchell, A, Gottfreid, J, Stocking, G, Walker, M and Fedeli, S. "Many Americans say made-up news is a critical problem that needs to be fixed." June 5, 2019. Pew Research Center. https://www.pewresearch.org/journalism/2019/06/05/many-americans-say-made-up-news-is-a-critical-problem-that-needs-to-be-fixed/

49 "Our Mission." https://www.factcheck.org/about/our-mission/

50 https://www.factcheck.org/2020/10/trumps-long-history-with-conspiracy-theories/

51 "The principles of the Truth-O-Meter: PolitiFact's methodology for independent fact-checking," October 27, 2020. https://www.politifact.com/article/2018/feb/12/principles-truth-o-meter-politifacts-methodology-i/#Truth-O-Meter%20ratings

52 Johnson, TM. "The FCC's authority to interpret Section 230 of the Communications Act." October 21, 2020. https://www.fcc.gov/news-events/blog/2020/10/21/fccs-authority-interpret-section-230-communications-act

53 Ruan, K. "Dear Congress: Platform accountability should not threaten online expression," October 27, 2020. https://www.aclu.org/news/free-speech/dear-congress-platform-accountability-should-not-threaten-online-expression

54 Ibid.

55 "Tech CEOs Senate testimony transcript." Rev, October 28, 2020. Retrieved from https://www.rev.com/blog/transcripts/tech-ceos-senate-testimony-transcript-october-28

56 Ibid.

57 Ibid.

58 Ibid.

59 Ibid.

60 Ibid.

61 "Breaking the News: Censorship, Suppression, and the 2020 Election." U.S. Committee on the Judiciary, November 17, 2020. https://www.judiciary.senate.gov/committee-activity/hearings/breaking-the-news-censorship-suppression-and-the-2020-election

62 Isaac, M., & Browning, K. "Zuckerberg and Dorsey face harsh questioning from lawmakers." The New York Times, January 6, 2021.

63 "Mark Zuckerberg & Jack Dorsey Testimony Transcript," (2020), op cit.

64 Ibid.

65 Full transcripts of these hearings are available at: "Mark Zuckerberg & Jack Dorsey Testimony Transcript Senate Tech Hearing November 17," https://www.rev.com/blog/transcripts/mark-zuckerberg-jack-dorsey-testimony-transcript-senate-tech-hearing-november-17 and recorded on Youtube: https://www.youtube.com/watch?v=9G6fvBxziNM

66 Ibid.

[67] Ibid.

[68] "Breaking the News: Censorship, Suppression, and the 2020 Election." U.S. Committee on the Judiciary, November 17, 2020. https://www.judiciary.senate.gov/committee-activity/hearings/breaking-the-news-censorship-suppression-and-the-2020-election

[69] Subsequent investigations and lawsuits revealed no evidence of substantial election fraud ("substantial" meaning that one or more fraudulent votes in a particular state would make any difference, either at the state or Federal level). For a complete list of lawsuits related to the 2020 presidential election, see https://www.americanbar.org/groups/public_interest/election_law/litigation/

[70] Rattner, N. "Trump's election lies were among his most popular tweets." CNBC, January 13, 2021. https://www.cnbc.com/2021/01/13/trump-tweets-legacy-of-lies-misinformation-distrust.html

[71] Hendel, J. "Facebook, Google and Twitter CEOs testifying again before Congress next month." Politico, February 18, 2021. https://www.politico.com/news/2021/02/18/facebook-google-twitter-congress-testify-469868

iCreate's Turnaround Proposal

Andrea Sutherland, University of Technology, Jamaica
Paul Golding, University of Technology, Jamaica
Lisa Facey-Shaw, University of Technology, Jamaica

On May 17, 2022, Tyrone Wilson, Chief Executive Officer (CEO) and President of iCreate Limited, a fledging creative training institute, needed to fundamentally pivot. The company had incurred losses since its inception in 2018 and had raised equity and borrowed funds to finance its operations. On December 31, 2021, accumulated losses totaled J$122.1 million.[1] Auditors had raised significant doubts about the company's ability to continue as a going concern, and some board members were in muted agreement. The prospect of Wilson losing control of the company, or worse, liquidation, loomed large.

In response, Wilson proposed a turnaround strategy in which a rights issue would be offered to shareholders to raise additional funds. The proceeds would be used to acquire an outdoor advertising company, in order to improve iCreate's bottom line. The plan also included restructuring the company into five divisions: training, advertising, media & entertainment, tech & e-commerce, and real estate. Wilson estimated that he could raise J$275 million, and the proceeds would be used for inter alia acquisition of a digital advertising company and repayment of debt. He estimated revenue growth of over J$470 million, and net profit was expected by Wilson to grow at a 3-year compound annual growth rate of approximately 16%. The additional capitalization from the rights issue would require that iCreate graduate from the Junior Stock Market (JSM) to the Main Market, with the implications being that iCreate would no longer be eligible for tax incentives associated with the JSM. The JSM was designed to encourage and promote investment in Jamaica's entrepreneurship community, and would allow investors to put capital into legitimate small and medium sized companies (SMEs) whose shares were traded on a special Jamaica Stock Exchange (JSE) platform.

Wilson wondered how the board would receive the rights issue. Were the projections too optimistic? The board meeting was scheduled for May 19, 2022, at 8:00am, two days away; he had little time to prepare, to be persuasive, and fine tune the details. He made a mental note that convincing the board would be the first hurdle. He would next need to convince the shareholders to subscribe to the rights issue. Based on the company's previous losses, would they?

WILSON'S ENTREPRENEURIAL JOURNEY

Wilson's first business began as a venture he undertook with his friends during his high school days. The group of friends saw and acted on a demand for spray-painted shirts during the season of one of Jamaica's premier athletic high school championships[2] that had long produced world-record sporting greats from Jamaica, such as world-recognized sprinters Usain Bolt and Shelly-Ann Fraser Pryce, two of the fastest athletes in the world.

After completing high school in 2004,[3] Wilson studied for a BSc. degree in banking and finance at the University of the West Indies (UWI) in Mona, Jamaica. While still a student, he became involved with several projects that gave him insights into the media and creative industries. Wilson explained that the projects included "writing for the *YouthLink* magazine of Jamaica's oldest newspaper," The Jamaica Gleaner.

In addition, he was Chair for the UWI Guild of Students' Publications Committee. Wilson enjoyed being involved with various aspects of the industry, including telling stories in written or video formats, writing various kinds of scripts, and the pre-press process. He decided that he wanted to start his own media company. Even though he was formally studying banking and finance, he was consumed with learning as much as he could about entrepreneurship, which led him to start working on his business plan.

iCREATE BACKGROUND

iCreate was formed in 2012 by eMedia Interactive Group Limited's founder, president & CEO, Tyrone Wilson, as a department within eMedia. Formerly eZines limited, eMedia Interactive Group Limited was a private company: a digital media and advertising business described as being powered by technology, creativity, and innovation. The company focused on developing contemporary ways to produce and distribute content for its clients and audiences through the firm's digital publications and videos.[4]

iCreate's goal was to offer skills training and work experience to young creatives and talented university students. However, over time, the functions of eMedia morphed into iCreate, with the latter being the focal point. In 2016, iCreate partnered with the University of the Commonwealth Caribbean (UCC), making the firm the official media institute of the University. The establishment of the iCreate Institute was welcomed by Dr. Winston Adams, executive chair of the University College of the Caribbean; Richard Byles, chair of the eMedia Interactive Group; and Renee Robinson, then Creative Industries Manager and Film Commissioner at Jamaica Promotions (JAMPRO). The positive response from these three individuals was based on iCreate's timely response to the demand for a trained, technology-skilled workforce in the creative sector.[5] In January 2018, iCreate was incorporated as a limited liability company. Just over a year later, on February 25, 2019, iCreate Limited issued an initial public offering (IPO) in which the firm netted J$56 million and was listed on the Junior Market of the Jamaica Stock Exchange (JSE). Proceeds of the IPO were targeted at providing funds for physical expansion and for the implementation of new training courses (see **Exhibit 1**: Company Highlights).

THE CREATIVE ECONOMY IN JAMAICA

Jamaica, a Caribbean nation with a population of approximately 2.8 million people in 2020, had struggled with the twin plights of high debt and low economic growth since its independence from Britain in 1962. In university, Wilson learned that the Jamaican economy was undiversified and heavily dependent on services, which accounted for more than 70% of gross domestic product (GDP). The country derived most of its foreign exchange from tourism, remittances, and bauxite/alumina. Jamaica had always excelled in sports (Usain Bolt) and music (Bob Marley), and Wilson thought that the creative industry would be a natural evolution for the Jamaican economy.

According to the United Nations Conference on Trade and Development (UNCTAD 2004), the creative economy was "an evolving concept which builds on the interplay between human creativity and ideas and intellectual property, knowledge and technology."[6] The HEART Trust/NTA, Jamaica's national skills training agency, conducted a Creative Industry study in 2017.[7] The study divided Jamaica's creative industry into nine sub-industries, namely animation, dance, fashion, music, film, literature & publishing, visual & graphic arts, media, and craft. While noting that there was limited available social and economic data on the creative industry, the study highlighted the linkages of the industry to other areas such as tourism (e.g. culture and festivals), information and communication technology/business process outsourcing (e.g. animation and gaming), and sport (e.g. sports apparel and journalism), among others.

The HEART study also recognized the growth of media channels, demand for content, increasing international support through agreements, and a widening of the regional market as opportunities which augured well for the creative industry. The potential threats included investment barriers, retention of talent, and reputational issues. The study suggested that significant training, such as in animation, content creation, dance, music, and film, was required if Jamaica's creative industry was to provide the employability skills needed to meet current and future workforce demands. The creative industry contributed 5.25% of Jamaica's GDP.

The HEART Trust/NTA (2017) study had specifically mentioned iCreate as a training provider of certificate courses in advertising, animation, content marketing & strategy, digital video production, and communications design. Two of the recommendations arising from the study were an increase in training capacity for several occupational areas in the industry (e.g. animators, content creators, and script writers) and the offering of programs in emerging areas such as storyboard creation and virtual reality development. Wilson pondered whether there was additional scope for course offerings in the industry, especially as iCreate had already expanded its offerings to include options in digital marketing and photography. Wilson needed to consider these emerging occupations for future growth.

Jamaica's government had undertaken several strategic initiatives that signaled the country's direction for economic growth in the creative industry. The initiatives included a revised culture policy, renamed as the National Policy on Culture and the Creative Economy, the activation of the National Cultural and Creative Industries Council, an e-Registry for entertainment and creative industries, UNESCO's listing of Jamaica's reggae music as a Global Cultural Treasure, and the listing of Kingston, Jamaica a UNESCO's Creative Cities Network.[8]

JAMAICA'S JUNIOR STOCK MARKET (JJSM)

Prior to 2009, it was very difficult for small and medium sized enterprises (SMEs) to raise capital through commercial loans, because they lacked the necessary security. Also, there was no capital market facility in Jamaica for SMEs to raise equity capital, which was considered extremely important in having a proper capital structure. This led to the proposal and implementation of the Junior Stock Exchange.[9] To stimulate economic growth, the Jamaican government, in collaboration with the Jamaica Stock Exchange (JSE) and other stakeholders, launched the Junior Market on April 1, 2009.

It was designed to encourage and promote investment in Jamaica's entrepreneurship, employment, and economic development. The Junior Market would allow investors to put capital into legitimate small and medium sized companies (SMEs), whose shares were traded on a special JSE platform.

When Wilson established iCreate in 2018 (See **Exhibit 1**: Company Highlights), he had targeted JJSM as the avenue for funding his new company. Wilson had considered the process to be listed on the JJSM as having been "complicated, with specified strict requirements," (see **Exhibit 2**: Requirements for Listing on the Junior Stock Exchange).

iCREATE'S 2019 IPO

Once the company was able to satisfy all of the JJSM requirements it was possible to raise capital via an IPO on the JJSM. iCreate's IPO opened at 9:00 a.m. on January 31, 2019, and closed at 4:00 p.m. on February 14, 2019. Within 36 hours after opening, the full share capital was taken up with subscriptions amounting to twice the J$70 million targeted from the market. After expenses, iCreate netted approximately J$56 million. Wilson commented, "I know that iCreate was on its way to being something special and growing into its own as a Company, but to see so many people participate is an indication of our capital market and also an indication of the brand iCreate."[10] iCreate intended to use the proceeds of the IPO to accomplish the following:

1. Acquire additional equipment, computers, and software to deliver courses.
2. Expand physical infrastructure to include additional computer labs, training rooms, and workshop space in Kingston and Montego Bay.
3. Implement new training courses such as certified professional diplomas, bachelor's degrees, and corporate training.
4. Pursue regional and international expansion.
5. Pay the expenses of the IPO, which the company estimated would not exceed J$12 million.

February 28, 2019 – the day iCreate was listed on the JJSM – "was a dream come true," Wilson recalled. "My family was there with me: my mother, father, brother, my wife . . . It felt really satisfying to reach that milestone, even though I knew it was just the beginning."

CHALLENGING POST IPO PERFORMANCE

After one year in operation, iCreate's financials at the end of 2019 depicted a company in crisis. Of the five IPO goals, the company achieved numbers one, two and five. The audited financials for December 31, 2019, indicated that the company grew its annual revenues to approximately J$45 million, but incurred a net loss of approximately J$46 million. iCreate closed its financial year with a weak balance sheet, including negative equity of J$4.98 million, due to losses that had piled up of about J$61 million. The company also recorded negative working capital (an excess of short-term liabilities over short-term assets) of J$33.5 million. The company's auditors raised significant doubts about its ability to continue as a going concern.

To fund working capital needs iCreate raised an additional J$24 million, through the issue of a bond arranged by Sagicor Investments Limited. The bond, issued on February 7, 2020, had semi-annual coupon payments of 12.5%, with a maturity date in five years. The loan was secured by present and future assets and property of the company.

In response to COVID-19 and associated financial pressures, iCreate embarked on a plan dubbed "Preserving Profits and Pivoting for Growth." The company moved all its classes online, closed its Montego Bay offices, laid off some staff, and reduced salaries. The former general manager and chief financial officer resigned, and to cut costs, they were not replaced. A new position of executive chair was also created to help to run the Company. The new executive chair, Jennifer Bailey, assumed the functions of general manager, Chief Operating Officer (COO) and Chief Financial Officer (CFO).

By the end of 2020, despite a tumultuous year, iCreate narrowed its losses to J$29M, compared with a loss of J$46M in 2019 (see **Exhibit 3**: Financial Statements 2021 - 2019). Auditors commented that revenue was not sufficient to avoid losses. iCreate's working capital position improved, but remained in deficit at J$22.98 million, while its accumulated losses jumped from J$61 million to nearly J$90 million.[11] The company also had mounting payables (liabilities due for payment in the short term increased from J$23.2 million to nearly J$30 million).

In 2021, iCreate raised additional capital through convertible loans of J$68 million, to help with its working capital needs. iCreate's losses, however, climbed to J$32 million compared with a loss of J$29 million in the prior year. The company had accumulated losses totaling J$122.1 million since its inception in 2018.

WILSON'S PROPOSAL

Wilson felt immense pressure in preparing for the board meeting and he wanted to be detailed, comprehensive, and strategic. In preparation, Wilson researched turnaround strategies. The first two of four strategies that he reviewed were cost efficiency and asset retrenchment. Wilson surmised that these two had been attempted by iCreate attempted under the "Preserving Profits and Pivoting for Growth" plan (described earlier). The third option focused on a company's core activities, and the final one was change of leadership. As a CEO, Wilson could not contemplate being pushed out of his own company, even though notable leaders like Apple's Steve Jobs had suffered this fate. His proposal to the board was therefore predicated on concentrating on expanded core activities. Wilson's plan was to offer the shareholders a rights issue, and use the proceeds to restructure and acquire a company that would help to improve the bottom line. In developing the plan, Wilson started with restructuring, acquisition, and finally determining how much would be required from the rights issue, to facilitate restructuring and acquisition.

Restructure
Wilson believed that for the company to grow it needed to diversify into other creative ventures. Wilson proposed a restructuring of the company to include five divisions: training, media & entertainment, advertising, tech & e-commerce, and real estate, which focused on building and developing "Creative City Real Estate" Projects. Wilson indicated that it was his position that these five divisions aligned with the strategic direction of iCreate, and would drive the basis of its expansion strategy (see **Exhibit 4** for the proposed new structure). Wilson also proposed two new executive positions: Group Chief Revenue Officer, which required someone with extensive experience in sales and digital advertising, and a Group Chief Financial Officer which required someone to oversee the financial activities.. To avoid conflict of interest and advance good governance, the position of board chair and CEO remained separate positions.

Acquisition

Wilson further proposed the acquisition of Visual Vibe.com Ltd. Visual Vibe.com Ltd. was a market leader in video board advertising in Jamaica. The company had enjoyed over sixteen years of success providing clients with high-impact video board advertising. Visual Vibe.com Ltd. had thirteen video boards island wide. There were eight spots in the capital, Kingston, with the remainder located in major towns such as Spanish Town, Portmore, Ocho Rios, Montego Bay, and Mandeville. Population data presented by STATIN indicated that Visual Vibe.com Ltd. covered 63.78% of the total population based on current locations. Wilson proposed that an opportunity existed for Visual Vibe.com Ltd. to tap into the remaining 36.22% of the population (see **Exhibit 5**, location of Visual Vibe.com Ltd. billboards).

Wilson proposed that Visual Vibe.com Ltd. would be governed by an independent board of directors which would consist of five directors. The company would be a subsidiary of iCreate and would be governed under the same principles and guidelines.

With the acquisition of Visual Vibe.com Ltd., revenue was expected to grow to J$477.5 million at a three-year Compound Annual Growth Rate (CAGR) of 22.9%. This growth in revenue would largely stem from Visual Vibe.com Ltd. (over 40%) and the expansion of other four divisions of iCreate. According to Wilson's plan, this growth in revenue was expected to assist iCreate in keeping the bottom line positive and growing. Net profit was expected to grow, at a three-year CAGR of 15.9%, to J$106 million (see **Exhibit 6** for Visual Vibe.com Ltd. Balance Sheet, Income Statement, and Cash flow for 2019 to 2021).

The 2021 Business Perception Survey for Jamaica's central bank, the Bank of Jamaica (BoJ), indicated that inflation for the subsequent twelve months was expected to be 9.8%, an increase relative to the previous survey out-turn of 8.9%. The BoJ out-turn for the Future Business Conditions Index mainly reflected an increase in the number of respondents of the view that conditions would be "worse."[12]

The out of home (OOH) advertising industry in Jamaica was very competitive. Visual Vibe.com Ltd.'s two main competitors were Caledonia Outdoor Advertising and iPrint Digital Ltd. Founded in 1993, Caledonia Outdoor Advertising was one of the largest outdoor advertising companies in Jamaica from Morant Point to Negril Point (one end of the island to the other), with more than 1,000 displays located in high traffic and valuable locations. Caledonia offered advertisers a diverse portfolio of billboards and outdoor solutions, for both local and international brands, that reached all demographic groups island-wide. Additionally, Caledonia owned the largest digital board on the island.

iPrint was a Jamaican-owned company, launched in 2006, with the aim of disrupting the print and signage industry. In 2018, it acquired the fifty-year-old billboard advertising agency National Outdoor Advertising Limited. iPrint was considered to be among the market leaders with over 800 advertising faces across the country in both physical and digital OOH advertising.

Rights Issue

Wilson proposed that the acquisition of Visual Vibe.com Ltd. would be funded by way of a pre-emptive renounceable rights issue to the existing ordinary stockholders (whose names appeared on the Register of Members at the close of business on the Record Date). The price proposed was $1.00 per share, in the proportion of 43 new ordinary shares for every 100 existing ordinary stock units then held by an existing ordinary stockholder. The offer would be open for seven calendar days. eMedia Limited, a private company owned and controlled by Wilson, was the single largest shareholder (see **Exhibit 7** for those holders on the register with the ten largest holdings of Existing

Ordinary Stock). iCreate stock was trading at J$3.77 on the date of record, May 17, 2022. Debt of $18.3M from Kintyre Holdings and $50.5M from Dequity Capital was converted to equity in early 2022 by the stockholders. Wilson was owner, founder, chair, and CEO of Kintyre Holdings.

Unlike a rights issue, in a typical share issue, the company would issue and sell additional shares to market participants, usually at a much higher price than a rights issue (i.e. at a lower discount). A typical share issue would dilute the current ownership of the existing owners because shares would be offered to the public at a discount. In addition, the share issuance fees were typically very high.

Wilson expected to raise J$275 million from the rights issue. He surmised that the proceeds would be used for (1) the acquisition of 100% of issued shares of Visual Vibe.com Ltd a privately held company, (2) the payment of transaction fees (estimated at J$30M), (3) the improvement of the digital screens in select locations, and (4) the repayment of a bond facility granted to the company in February 2020.

Wilson noted that the rights issue would exceed the maximum allowable business capitalization required to remain on the Junior Stock Market. Therefore, iCreate would need to graduate to the main market of the Jamaica Stock Exchange. Graduating to the main market would mean that the ten-year tax incentive granted to companies on the Junior market would no longer apply. Should the rights issue resolution pass both the board and the shareholders, immediately following the closing of the offer iCreate would be required to make an application to the Jamaica Stock Exchange for the listing of the additional stock units arising from the rights issue.

CONVINCING THE BOARD

The board consisted of eight people, including Wilson. The skill sets of the members were varied, including strategic management, marketing and communication, auditing and accounting, finance, and entrepreneurship. Each member had more than ten years of experience in their respective areas. Except for Wilson, only one other member of the board was a shareholder (Dequity Capital, with 25.29% of issued shares). Wilson had floated the restructuring idea in a previous meeting to gauge the reactions of board members. The response was mixed: a few members were eager while others were more skeptical. Wilson expected a tough interrogation from the board, especially relating to the he plausibility of the growth rate of 22.9% per annum in an economy which was projected to grow at 1% in 2023, and a creative sector which contributed 5.25% in GDP. Questions would be raised about how an injection of capital could force the Company to list on the main JSE market, and lose the benefits of being on the Junior Market. after only three years. Consequently, the seven years' worth of tax incentives if iCreate graduated to the main market would be lost.

Wilson remained passionate and optimistic about the future of iCreate, despite its financial problems and the continued "going concern" doubt raised by the auditors. It was not lost on Wilson that the proposal was existential for his company. The board was the first hurdle in the turnaround strategy; if he was successful in convincing the board, he would need to convince the shareholders to subscribe to the offer. Convincing the shareholders was not a foregone conclusion, given iCreate's previous performance. At both the board meeting and the possible subsequent shareholder's meeting, an ordinary resolution (more than 50% of shareholder votes) was required to pass the proposal. Wilson thought, one hurdle at a time, one at a time.

Exhibit 1 - Company Highlights

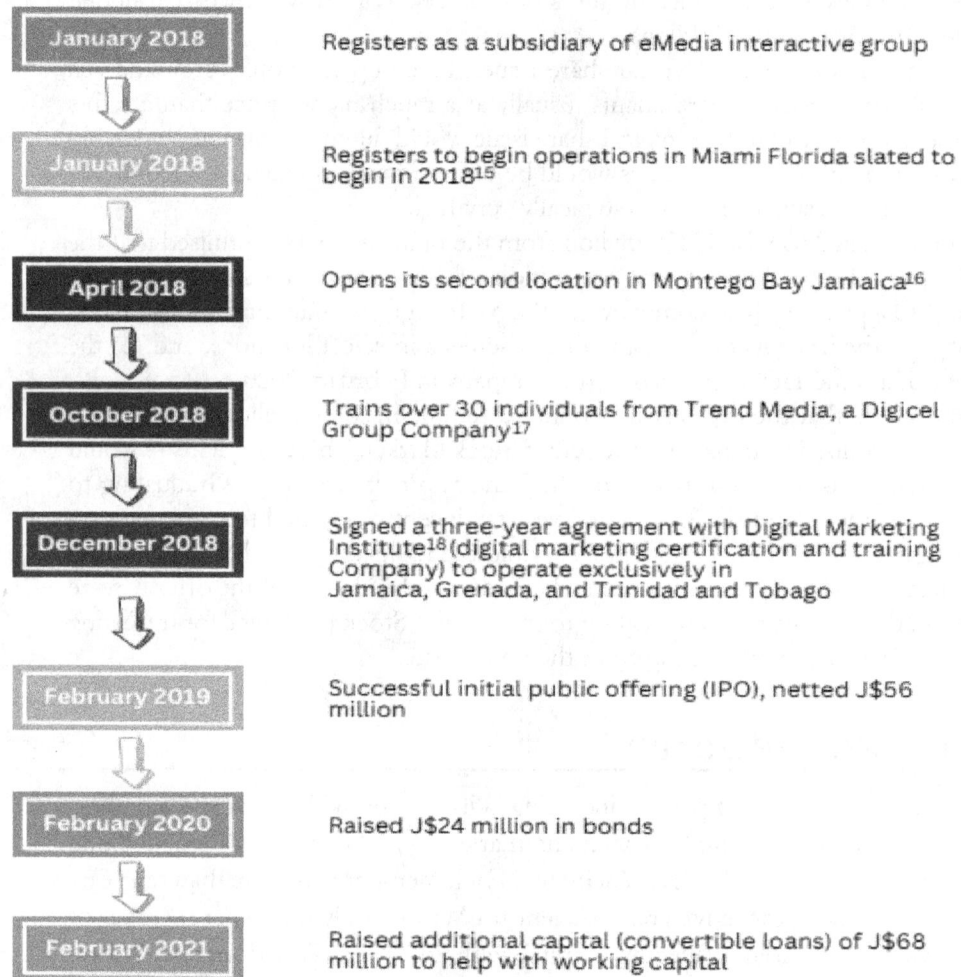

January 2018	Registers as a subsidiary of eMedia interactive group
January 2018	Registers to begin operations in Miami Florida slated to begin in 2018[15]
April 2018	Opens its second location in Montego Bay Jamaica[16]
October 2018	Trains over 30 individuals from Trend Media, a Digicel Group Company[17]
December 2018	Signed a three-year agreement with Digital Marketing Institute[18] (digital marketing certification and training Company) to operate exclusively in Jamaica, Grenada, and Trinidad and Tobago
February 2019	Successful initial public offering (IPO), netted J$56 million
February 2020	Raised J$24 million in bonds
February 2021	Raised additional capital (convertible loans) of J$68 million to help with working capital

[15]This was in anticipation of going public and rapid expansion
[16]Montego Bay offices was opened in anticipation of expansion and were primarily for classes. This office was closed in 2020 due to the effects of COVID-19 and the migration of classes online
[17]Trend Media is a digital media and strategy company providing expertise for advertisers to impact their audiences across platforms. Providing for this company was a test bed for ICreate strategy.
[18]The Digital Marketing Institute is a global organization which offers certification in digital marketing. iCreate is an exclusive Partner which offers this certification.

Source: iCreate

Exhibit 2 - Requirements for Listing on the Junior Stock Exchange

The Jamaica Stock Exchange lists some requirements for consideration to be listed on the Junior Stock Exchange. These include:

General Requirements for Listing

Companies desirous of listing on the Junior Market must do so via an Initial Public Offering, requiring the issue of a prospectus complying with the Companies Act and the Securities Act.

The SME must appoint a mentor to its board. The mentor must be approved as 'Fit & Proper' by the Financial Services Commission (FSC).

The JSE's general scrutiny of the SME, for the purposes of graduation to the main board of the Exchange, is a requirement during the period where the SME is listed on the Junior Market.

Minimum Issued Capital and Number of Stockholders

The shareholder's equity of the company following the capital-raising activity outlined in the prospectus shall not be less than J$50 million and shall not exceed J$500 million. All securities which are the subject of the company's request for listing must be issued and fully paid at the date of the application to the Exchange.

The company must have a minimum of 25 shareholders holding not less than 20% of the issued share capital.

Any company listed on the Junior Market that fails to maintain the minimum capital requirement and the minimum number of shareholders stipulated above shall be delisted.

Taxation Issues

The taxation support includes a tax incentive for an allowable period not exceeding ten (10) years from the date of listing on the JSE Junior Market, to be implemented as follows:

> A full income tax holiday for half of the Allowed Incentive Period after listing
> A half income tax holiday for the second half of the Allowed Incentive

Period

> An exemption from tax on dividends or other distributions by Junior Market

companies.

If a company exceeds its maximum shareholder's equity capital capitalization of J$500 million, it is required to list on the main JSE Board. If the company delists within 15 years of being listed on the combined Junior Market and main exchanges it will be required to repay, to the Government, the tax benefits enjoyed during this period.

Source: Jamaica Stock Exchange

Exhibit 3 - iCreate Audited Financial Statement 2021 - 2018.

Audited Statement of Financial Position December 2021- 2018

	31-Dec-21	31-Dec-20	31-Dec-19	31-Dec-18
Fixed Assets	**13,599,586.00**	**21,641,075.00**	**28,850,453.00**	**7,419,655.00**
Current Assets				
Trade and other receivables	7,376,515.00	7,458,337.00	2,126,183.00	5,373,063.00
Due from related party	7,465,091.00	6,547,098.00	8,458,653.00	1,756,054.00
Cash and other bank balances	47,116,587.00	708,599.00	3,241,547.00	269,090.00
Total Current Assets	61,958,193.00	14,714,034.00	13,826,383.00	7,398,207.00
Total Assets	**75,557,779.00**	**36,355,109.00**	**42,676,836.00**	**14,817,862.00**
Current Liabilities	37,516,471.00	37,697,243.00	47,369,682.00	29,165,917.00
Long Term Liabilities	28,479,433.00	25,633,693.00	289,215.00	-
Equity	9,561,875.00	(26,975,827.00)	(4,982,061.00)	(14,348,055.00)
Total Liability & Equity	75,557,779.00	36,355,109.00	42,676,836.00	**14,817,862.00**
Profit and Loss				
Revenues	32,826,894.00	58,377,536.00	46,158,213.00	31,848,759.00
Direct Expenses	8,340,284.00	22,132,816.00	24,116,780.00	11,839,112.00
Gross Profit	**24,486,610.00**	**36,244,720.00**	**22,041,433.00**	**20,009,647.00**
Other Income	**5,326,929.00**	**34,985.00**	**559,258.00**	**119,790.00**
Administrative and general expenses	48,846,659.00	45,938,260.00	51,901,753.00	32,058,845.00
EBITDA	**(19,033,120.00)**	**(9,658,555.00)**	**(29,301,062.00)**	**(11,929,408.00)**
Depreciation	3,336,165.00	3,986,852.00	3,177,366.00	1,045,093.00
EBIT	**(22,369,285.00)**	**(13,645,407.00)**	**(32,478,428.00)**	**(12,974,501.00)**
Finance costs	9,893,013.00	15,419,306.00	12,961,526.00	2,094,461.00
EBT	**(32,262,298.00)**	**(29,064,713.00)**	**(45,439,954.00)**	**(15,068,962.00)**
Taxation (Expense)/Credit	-0-	-0-	(510,122.00)	220,907.00
Surplus from license, other comprehensive for the year	-0-	7,070,947.00	-	-0-
Total Comprehensive Income (Loss)	**(32,262,298.00)**	**(21,993,766.00)**	**(45,950,076.00)**	**(14,848,055.00)**

Source: Jamaica Stock Exchange

Exhibit 3 - iCreate Audited Financial Statement 2021 – 2018 (Cont'd)

Statement of Cash Flows 2021 – 2019

Cash Flows from Operating Activities	2021	2020	2019
Net Loss for the year	**(32,262,298)**	**(29,064,713)**	**(45,950,076)**
Adjustment for Items not affecting cash			
Depreciation and amortisation	3,336,165	3,986,852	3,177,366
Depreciation charge on right-of-use asset	554,568	6,943,644	10,120,786
Right of use interest expense	3,742	330,323	990,385
Derecognition of leasehold improvements	4,576,709	3,640,714	-
Expected credit loss provision	8,532,563	3,796,795	8,796,969
Surplus from licence	-0-	7,070,947	-
Interest expense	8,748,572	7,457,198	-
Deferred taxation	-	-	510,122
Amortization adjustment, net	(202,256)		
(Increase) / Decrease in operating assets:	**(6,712,235)**	**4,161,760**	**(22,354,448)**
Trade and other receivables			
Due from related party	(8,450,741)	(9,128,949)	(5,550,088)
Increase / (decrease) in operating liabilities:	**(910,345)**	**1,911,556**	**(4,921,663)**
Trade and other payables			
Customer deposits	1,785,523	4,770,882	13,738,975
Cash used in operating activities	-	(890,000)	(160,000)
Interest Paid	(14,287,798)	825,249	(19,247,224)
Net cash used in operating activities	(8,748,572)	(5,768,818)	-
Cash Flows from Investing Activities	**(23,036,370)**	**(4,943,569)**	**(19,247,224)**
Acquisition of property, plant and equipment			
Acquisition of intangible assets	-	(206,285)	(17,330,860)
Net cash used in investing activities	(223,696)	(7,155,547)	-
Cash Flows from Financing Activities	**(223,696)**	**(7,361,832)**	**(17,330,860)**
Lease payments, net			
Issued share capital, net	(612,618)	(7,500,413)	(10,830,419)
Paid-in-capital	-	-	55,316,070
Loan proceeds	68,800,000	-	-
Loan repayments	6,066,674	31,900,000	-
Convertible notes	(4,259,108)	(2,535,522)	-
Net cash provided by financing activities	-	-	(17,500,000)
Net Increase / (Decrease) In Cash and Bank Balances	**69,994,948**	**21,864,065**	**26,985,651**
Opening Cash and Bank Balances	**46,734,882**	**9,558,664**	**(9,592,433)**
Closing Cash and Bank Balances	**235,321**	**(9,323,343)**	**269,090**
Represented By:	**46,970,203**	**235,321**	**(9,323,343)**
Cash and bank deposits			
Bank overdraft	47,116,587	708,599	3,241,547
	(146,384)	(473,278)	(12,564,890)
	46,970,203	**235,321**	**(9,323,343)**

Source: Jamaica Stock Exchange

Exhibit 4 - Proposed New Company Structure

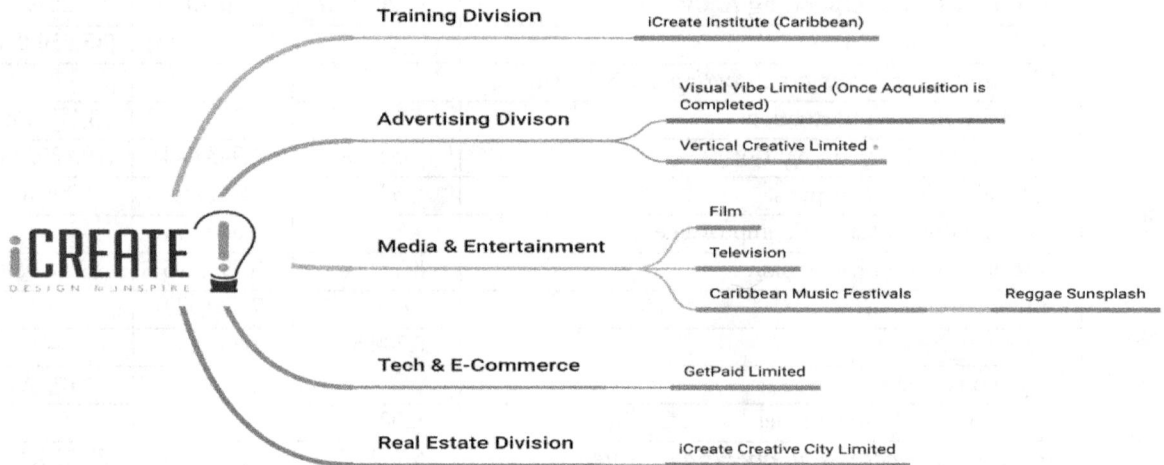

iCreate Division	Entity
Training Division	iCreate Institute (Caribbean)
Advertising Divison	Visual Vibe Limited (Once Acquisition is Completed) / Vertical Creative Limited
Media & Entertainment	Film / Television / Caribbean Music Festivals — Reggae Sunsplash
Tech & E-Commerce	GetPaid Limited
Real Estate Division	iCreate Creative City Limited

Source: iCreate

Exhibit 5 - Location of Visual Vibe.com Ltd. Billboards

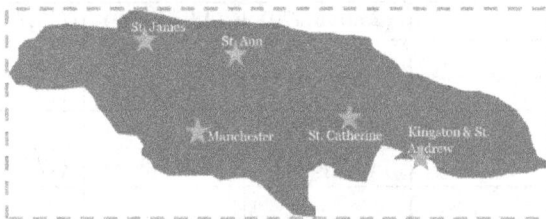

The billboards are strategically placed, large, full colour, high resolution, with crystal clear display screens. The company has thirteen (13) videoboards installed in key strategic locations island-wide.

Location/Site Ownership:

- *Government owned sites:* Visual Vibe is required to pay an annual fee to the Kingston St. Andrew Municipal Corporation ('KSAMC') or other Parish Council Authorities to be compliant.

- *Non-Government owned:* Visual Vibe is required to pay an annual license fee with an additional payment to the property owner and benefit of free ADS on a monthly basis as part of the compensation package.

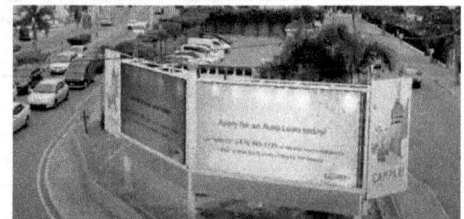

Median on Knutsford Boulevard

Parish	Location
Kingston & St. Andrew	1. Mandela Park, Half-Way-Tree 2. Discount Pharmacy Parking Lot, Manor Park 3. Ranny Williams Entertainment Centre, Hope Road 4. NCB Parking Lot, New Kingston 5. Median on Knutsford Boulevard 6. Cross Roads 7. Captain's Bakery, North Parade 8. Emancipation Park
St. Catherine	9. Intersection of March Pen Road and Burke Road, Spanish Town 10. Portmore Town Centre
St. Ann	11. Turtle River Park, Ocho Rios
St. James	12. Intersection of Gloucester Avenue and Queen's Drive, Montego Bay
Manchester	13. Mandeville Market, Mandeville

Source: iCreate

Exhibit 6 - Visual Vibe.com Ltd Financials 2021 - 2019

Visual Vibe.com Limited

Audited Statement of Financial Position December 2021- 2019

	Dec 31, 2021	Dec 31, 2020	Dec 31, 2019
Fixed Assets	102,917,529	105,714,038	157,100,783
Current Assets	17,144,601	25,223,516	22,976,258
Total	120,062,130	130,937,554	180,077,041
Current Liabilities	5,319,541	2,548,641	14,748,561
Long Term Liabilities & areholders' Equity	114,742,589	128,388,913	165,328,480
Total Liability & Equity	120,062,130	130,937,554	180,077,041

Profit and Loss

	Dec 31, 2021	Dec 31 2020	Dec 31, 2019
Revenues	142,609,951	144,220,105	160,680,273
Direct Expenses	(33,097,927)	(32,457,111)	(36,614,631)
Gross Profit	109,512,024	(111,762,994	124,065,642
Expenses	(54,713,366)	(58,397,510)	(56,526,707)
Profit/(loss) Before Tax and Finance	54,798,658	53,365,484	67,538,935
Net finance cost	(1,183,204)	(1,684,574)	(1,800,205)
Profit/(loss) Before Tax	53,615,454	51,680,910	65,738,730
Taxation Expense	-0-	-0-	(11,482,913)
Total Comprehensive Income (Loss)	53,615,454	51,680,910	54,255,817

Source: iCreate

Exhibit 6 - Visual Vibe.com Ltd Financials 2021 – 2019 (Cont'd)

Visual Vibe.com Limited: Statement of Cash Flows

Cash Flows From Operating Activities	2021	2020	2019
Net Profit For The Year	**53,615,454**	**51,680,910**	**54,255,817**
Adjustment For Items Not Affecting Cash			
Depreciation And Amortisation	15,296,509	23,102,027	**22,674,922**
Interest Income	(8,599)	(10,840)	**(26,467)**
Taxation Write-Back	0	10,192,205	**11,482,913**
Interest Expense	1,055,810	1,234,382	**1,401,686**
	69,959,174	**86,198,684**	**89,788,871**
(Increase) / Decrease In Operating Assets:			
Accounts Receivables	7,695,149	(3,665,912)	**(13,039,192)**
Other Receivables	(826,676)	350,173	1,004,264
Accounts Payable And Accrued Charges	642,618	(912,593)	1,516,770
Cash Generated From Operating Expenses	77,470,265	81,970,352	46,438,810
Taxation Paid Deducted At Source	0	11,335,216	(4,959,704)
Net Cash Used In Operating Activities	**77,470,265**	**70,635,136**	**41,479,106**
Cash Flows rrom Investing Activities			
Acquisition Of Property, Plant And Equipment	12,500,000	4,564,486	(40,328,950)
Interest Received	8,599	10,840	26,467
Net Cash Used In Investing Activities	**12,491,401**	**4,553,646**	**(40,302,483)**
Cash Flows from Financing Activities			
Interest Paid	(1,055,810)	(1,234,382)	(1,401,686)
New Loan Proceeds	12,500,000	0	0
Loan Repaid	(4,713,496)	(1,892,842)	(2,098,246)
Dividends	(72,920,000)	(64,022,747	0
Net Cash Provided By Financing Activities	**(66,189,306)**	**(67,149,971)**	**(3,499,932)**
Net Increase/(Decrease) In Cash and Bank Balances	**(1,210,442)**	**(1,068,481)**	**(2,323,309)**
Opening Cash and Bank Balances	**9,979,964**	**11,048,445**	**13,371,754**
Closing Cash and Bank Balances	**8,769,522**	**9,979,964**	**11,084,445**
Represented By:			
Cash And Bank Deposits	**8,769,522**	**9,979,964**	**11,048,445**

Source: iCreate

Exhibit 7 - Top 10 Shareholdings for iCreate Limited Ordinary Shares

As at Proposed time.	Number of shares	% of total
eMedia Interactive Group Limited	100,000,000	32.4086
Dequity Capital Management Limited	78,054,167	25.2962
Kintyre Holdings Limited	29,516,129	9.5658
Sagicor Investments Jamaica Limited	17,470,147	5.6618
Andrew Pairman	14,269,314	4.6245
Dane Warren	8,167,962	2.6471
Guardsman Group Limited	2,000,000	0.6482
Kerry-Ann Spencer	2,000,000	0.6482
Jevaughn Clarke	1,526,200	0.4946
Mesha-Gay Mattis	1,435,343	0.54652

Total Issued Capital: 308,560,242
Total units owned by top 10 shareholders: 255,839,353
Total percentage owned by top 10 shareholders: 82.9139%

Source: iCreate/Jamaica Stock Exchange

NOTES

[1] US$1 = J$154.71
[2] Your Best U - Tyrone Wilson -
https://www.youtube.com/watch?v=K61ER83E9_w
[3] https://cioviews.com/tyrone-wilson-empowering-the-jamaican-community-with-icreate-institute/
[4] https://www.linkedin.com/Company/emedia-interactive-limited/about/
[5] https://dobusinessjamaica.com/news/2016/10/5252/
[6] https://unctad.org/topic/trade-analysis/creative-economy-programme
[7] HEART Trust/NTA (2017). Creative Industry Study. Retrieved January 25, 2021 from https://lmip.heart-nsta.org/Publications.aspx
[8] https://en.unesco.org/creativity/governance/periodic-reports/submission/4763
[9] https://www.jamstockex.com/investor-centre/junior-market-information
[10] http://jamaica-gleaner.com/article/business/20190313/icreate-looks-global-horizons-ipo-cash#:~:text=Armed%20with%20%2470%20million%20from,Miami%20to%20other%20markets%20overseas
[11] https://jamaica-gleaner.com/article/business/20210908/icreate-auditors-raise-concern-about-revenue-generation
[12] https://boj.org.jm/wp-content/uploads/2022/02/Inflation-Expectations-Survey-December-2021_Final.pdf

Caged or Cage-Free?

Karen E. Boroff, Seton Hall University
Karen Meleta, Guest Lecturer, Seton Hall University
Paula Becker Alexander, Seton Hall University

It was an October Monday morning in 2019 when Mel Mathers,[1] chief sustainability officer of the Independent Food Retailers Consortium (IFRC) – a cooperative buying group that served independent grocery retailers – sat down at his desk to tackle his morning email. At first glance he thought his company's email system was experiencing a glitch, when he saw his inbox registering an unprecedented 10,000 unread emails. As he began to scroll through his inbox, the email subject line was all the same: "Please take decisive action now!" Mathers opened the first email and began to read:

> I was horrified to learn that your stores sell eggs from hens confined to cages. Hens should not suffer in cages where they cannot spread their wings, walk, or engage in their normal behavior. The confinement is inhumane. Many supermarkets have pledged to stop selling eggs from hens in cages – it's time IFRC does the same. I will not shop in your Kansas City store if you continue to sell eggs from hens in cages.

One after another, all the emails were exactly the same, and many referenced locations across the nation where IFRC did not have stores. Mathers quickly concluded that these weren't IFRC customers who were writing; the emails were form letters, a campaign likely promoted by an animal rights group. In Mathers' 25-year career working in corporate philanthropy and social responsibility, he had not seen such a well-coordinated campaign from a Non-government Organization (NGO), though the role of those who had corporate social responsibility (CSR) under their responsibilities had changed dramatically in as many years. In his early career, Mathers' work focused on charitable giving and conservation programs that reduced the company's impact on the environment or reduced risk. But nowadays, he believed that today's CSR practitioners had to concern themselves with societal issues that went far beyond the company's core competency or sphere of influence.

Mathers wasn't the only one who had received the emails that morning. All the IFRC executive board members, including the chairman of the board, had their inboxes filled with these emails of the campaign.

Following the flood of emails, Mathers received a message from the leader of a national animal rights group demanding that IFRC make a pledge to transition all of its egg supply to cage-free production. Another email from the animal rights group claimed it would appear at the annual meetings of those IFRC members that were publicly traded, to protest the selling of conventional caged eggs. That member-owner was particularly upset about facing boycotts, pickets, and bad publicity and told Mathers exactly that.

By 10:00 that morning, the call came from the company CEO instructing Mathers to present a brief to the board on Friday. The CEO noted that Mathers should be prepared to make a recommendation as to whether IFRC members should make a public pledge to transition to selling only cage-free eggs in its stores (including a timeline for doing so), or continue offering its customers a choice, selling both caged and cage-free eggs. "Four days was not a lot of time to finalize a recommendation," he uttered to himself.

THE INDEPENDENT FOOD RETAILERS CONSORTIUM

With an average one to two percent profit margin, it was increasingly difficult for small 'mom-and-pop' grocery stores to compete with multi-national food chains. The economies of scale achieved by big box and online retailers enabled them to secure the best prices from suppliers and lower their overall cost of operations. To improve their bargaining power, many smaller independent grocers joined together to form cooperatives such as the Independent Food Retailers Consortium (IFRC).[2]

IFRC handled all product procurement on behalf of its member stores, from produce and dairy products to canned goods, paper supplies, baking needs, breads, and more. Member stores stocked private label and nationally branded products (e.g. cereals from General Mills or Kellogg, Skippy peanut butter, etc.). IFRC procured more than 50,000 SKU (stock-keeping unit) items for its members and handled the warehousing and distribution of these goods as well. Independent grocers retained their own ownership and control of store operations: expanding or renovating stores, hiring, and promoting personnel. As part of the founding agreement when this food cooperative was formed, grocery store members specifically preserved their independence and the critical importance of being a local grocery store that could meet the specific needs of the communities the stores served, including ethnic foods and natural and organic items. IFRC members prided themselves on offering its customers choices in all categories, including value-priced items for its low-income consumers. Hundreds of independent grocers were members of IFRC, owning more than 1000 grocery stores among them. Although the vast majority of IFRC members were privately held small businesses, several of its members were publicly traded companies owning multiple stores.

While the members controlled their stores, each had IFRC somewhere in their store name. A store located in Springfield, MA was called "Springfield IFRC"; one doing business in Canton, OH bore the name "IFRC Canton." IFRC's logo was unique and identifiable, both in the store names and on IFRC private label products (cans of peas, ketchup bottles, milk, and more). Because of the shared brand name, IFRC corporate staff handled issues that could impact the brand's reputation and managed public affairs on behalf of its members.

The average IFRC store customer had a household income about $74,000 a year (on par with the U.S. national average). As a comparison, Mathers knew that Amazon and Whole Foods Market shoppers had median household incomes, respectively, of $90,100 and $95,200 in 2017.[3] For IFRC stores, household incomes varied widely from community to community. Some communities fell below the national average by 40-50 percent. Many IFRC members were committed to opening stores in "food deserts," historically underserved communities that lacked access to affordable, nutritious, and fresh foods. In urban areas, a food desert was defined as a low-income community without access to a supermarket within one mile. In rural communities, food desert residents had no supermarket within ten miles. According to the U.S. Department of Agriculture, as of 2017 nearly 39.5 million Americans (12.8% of the U.S. population) lived in food deserts.[4]

Mathers turned his attention to examining IRFC's policies to see if these could illuminate the decision as to whether or not to make the pledge demanded by the activists.

IFRC's MISSION AND CORPORATE SOCIAL RESPONSIBILITY STATEMENT

Mathers reflected on his role in CSR over the years. He believed that his job responsibilities had widened as a CSR manager, so prepared himself for the expanding role by attending courses and conferences, and had educated himself on a broad range of sustainability issues including sustainable sourcing, animal welfare, lifecycle analysis, and other climate related issues. At the same time, there was an obligation to be a fiduciary of IFRC, as he had a financial obligation to serve in the best interests of IFRC. In turn, Mathers was worried about how the email campaign cited other retailers, restaurants, and food service companies who had made the commitment to transition to cage-free eggs by 2025 or sooner; the email campaign writers had accompanied their demand with threats to boycott or stage demonstrations at its members' stores, potentially impacting the financial success of these stores.

The IFRC mission was to ensure the success of its independent grocers and provide them with the necessary technology and marketing tools to succeed in a competitive marketplace. This goal was especially vital to the independent grocer in 2019 as competitors such as Walmart and Costco, discounters such as Aldi and Trader Joe's, and pure "online" retailers, such as Amazon with its Whole Foods ownership, often had a price advantage, made significant investments in marketing outreach, and touted their philanthropy and social impact as a reason to shop with them.

In preparing his brief for the board of directors, Mathers turned to IFRC's corporate social responsibility statement (CSR) for guidance.

> IFRC's members are committed to making a meaningful impact in its communities through its philanthropy and volunteer activities, reducing its environmental footprint through the daily actions and business decisions it makes; it ensures the well-being and safety of its associates and deliver to its customers nutritious, fresh foods at affordable prices in an enjoyable shopping experience. We encourage our colleagues to promote sustainable business practices in each of their individual roles and areas of responsibility.

Mathers noted two aspects of its CSR statement that were applicable in this situation and could conflict with going 100 percent cage-free: reducing its environmental footprint and keeping food affordable for its customers. Mathers knew that cage-free eggs sold for as much as four times more than conventional caged eggs, and were likely to be unaffordable for many low-income customers. He also recalled a study that compared the environmental impacts of the varying housing systems. "We are committed to making science-based decisions – I'll need to present all of this information to the board so they can make an informed decision."

MATERIALITY ASSESSMENT AT IFRC

As he began to outline his presentation to the IFRC board of directors, Mathers pulled out the materiality assessment that IFRC had performed a year or so earlier, to get a perspective on IFRC's stakeholders' view of animal welfare issues (See **Exhibit 1**). The assessment was a tool to evaluate the impact a given issue would have on IFRC's financial well-being against that same issue's importance to IFRC's stakeholders. The plot points on the materiality assessment chart were made through a series of interviews and surveys with IFRC's various stakeholders, including members of its board of directors, the consortium members it served, and its suppliers, employees, and customers.

Mathers examined the chart. "Animal welfare was not as impactful, relative to other areas, when this chart was developed," he saw. Yet Mathers knew that IFRC had a long-standing and well-developed animal welfare policy for a dozen species in its food supply chain, including egg-laying hens, which had been put in place years before any materiality chart was fashioned. That policy had five basic freedoms for animals:

- Freedom from hunger and thirst
- Freedom from discomfort
- Freedom from pain, injury, or disease
- Freedom to express most normal behaviors
- Freedom from fear and distress

The standards, developed with the assistance of veterinarians, were based on science and animal husbandry best practices. The policy required that animals were handled in a humane manner through all phases of production. For hens, this included housing and transportation. All of its suppliers were obligated to include the following statement in their employee training: "the willful and intentional abuse of animals will not be tolerated." Mathers knew that these freedoms included, for egg-laying hens, standards on flock health, nutrition, feed, and water, and set minimum requirements for cage space allowance.

Mathers was unsettled with IFRC's financial materiality assessment. "Our financial materiality assessment places animal welfare as not as impactful, but IFRC had a long-standing strong animal welfare policy, way before we even discussed materiality. Shouldn't these mesh with each other?," he asked himself. Mathers was aware that organizations were moving beyond financial materiality charts to one called "double materiality."[5] Here, both financial materiality and environmental and social impacts were plotted. He learned that there was also "dynamic materiality." Here, materiality assessment was considered a process, changing constantly, depending on events in a firm's business environment and driving forces that may necessitate a reordering of strategies.[6] One paper posited that there may well be positive but non-measurable impacts for society even without a business case behind the decision.[7] "We have not begun to probe into these new forms of materiality," Mathers admitted to himself.

EGG PRODUCTION SYSTEM

The US was a major egg producer.[8] In 2018, the economic impact of the U.S. egg industry was nearly $30 billion; that number was expected to grow to almost $35 billion in 2020.[9] The average wage earned by an employee in the industry was about $56,000 annually, plus benefits. The top three egg-producing states were Iowa, Ohio, and Indiana.[10]

Mathers turned his attention to educating himself more comprehensively on how eggs were produced. There were four broad categories of egg production housing methods, with variations in each.[11] These were:

1. The conventional or caged or battery method
2. The enriched caged colony method
3. The cage-free or free-run aviary method
4. The free-range or pasture-raised method

Each category described the environment in which the hen was raised, housed, and laid her eggs. For each method, standards were generally set by animal husbandry experts, defining the best practices to ensure food safety, worker well-being, and animal welfare, and to reduce environmental impact.

With the first three methods, the hens' housing, and their ability to engage in their natural behavior varied greatly. The differences of these categories allowed egg producers to label their product accordingly. Often, they charged a premium for the product based on the method used. The premium reflected the additional operating costs incurred from using different housing systems, including higher feed costs for cage-free birds than non-cage-free, capital costs, labor costs, real estate costs, and depreciation expenses associated with building new cage-free systems. Mathers made a chart comparing the percentage cost difference between conventional vs. cage-free methods, which he gathered from inquiries and readings.

Operational Input	Percent higher that cage-free was over conventional (caged) methods
Feed	13.8% higher
Wages of employees	232% higher
Pullet rearing	210% higher
Depreciation of buildings / equipment	160% higher
Repairs, utilities, supplies, etc.	100% higher

In the conventional or caged egg production systems, hens were housed in cages tiered on top of one another in the production facility (see **Exhibit 2, Figure 1** for an illustration). Introduced in the 1950s, the system was designed to protect flocks from weather, predators, and disease, and gave them better access to standardized nutrition.[12] This housing system curtailed the natural aggressive and dangerous pecking behavior exhibited by hens, the latter of which resulted in higher mortality rates among flocks.[13] Mathers learned that caged hens had fewer pecking related deaths than hens in cage-free systems, which resulted in lower hen mortality rates when compared to cage-free systems. One study reported that "larger hens in a flock will often peck to death the smaller, weaker ones."[14] Usually 4 to 6 hens shared a cage; each hen had about 67 square inches of space. Critics pointed out that these caged birds could not exhibit natural behavior including perching and dustbathing. Mathers read a short item published by the Humane Society:

The worst torture to which a battery (caged) hen is exposed is the inability to retire somewhere for the act of laying. For the person who knows something about animals it is truly heart-rending to watch how a chicken tries again and again to crawl beneath her fellow cagemates to search there in vain for cover.[15]

The enriched caged colony housing was the second housing method. In this setting, hens in groups of 6 to 8 were raised together in larger space, with room to perch and with separate nesting areas. Proponents argued that with greater freedom of movement, hens exhibited more natural behaviors, but still protected flocks from diseases(see **Exhibit 2, Figure 2** for an illustration.)

The third housing system was the cage-free or free-run aviary system, where nests were available for laying eggs, and hens were free to fly, perch, roam, and dustbathe (see **Exhibit 2, Figure 3** for an illustration). In the fourth system, free-range, hens were also cage-free. However, free-range required that producers let the hens roam freely in a barn or, in the case of "pasture-raised" free-range, hens had to have access to the outdoors.

Mathers also learned about "speciests," people, according to animal rights activists, who did not believe that animals should have the same rights as humans.[16] Mathers made a rough sketch of the four systems for himself based on hen freedom, even though hens had a natural tendency to crowd or flock with each other, no matter the space given to all the hens.

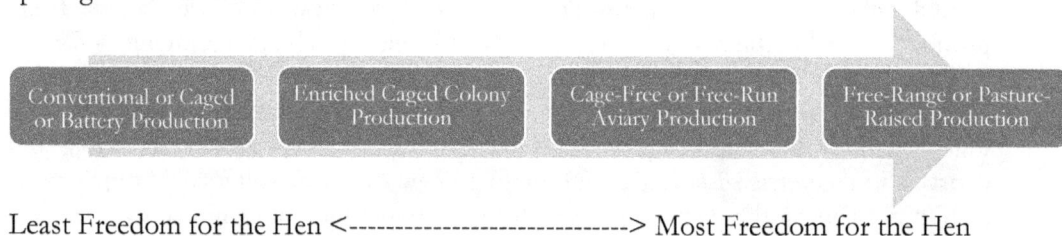

| Conventional or Caged or Battery Production | Enriched Caged Colony Production | Cage-Free or Free-Run Aviary Production | Free-Range or Pasture-Raised Production |

Least Freedom for the Hen <------------------------------> Most Freedom for the Hen

Animal rights activists strongly preferred cage-free production systems. The United States Department of Agriculture (USDA) required that eggs labeled as cage-free had to be produced by hens housed in a building, room, or enclosed area that allowed for unlimited access to food and water, and that provided the freedom to roam within the area during the laying cycle.[17] In cage-free designs, hens could scratch for food and search for water. They were free to fly, perch, roam, and dustbathe. They could select where they wished to nest to lay eggs, more in keeping with their natural behavior while providing a sense of security in nesting and laying eggs.[18]

Some states, such as Colorado, Washington, Oregon, Michigan, and Utah, had passed legislation prohibiting the sale of caged eggs entirely.[19] Several non-governmental organizations (NGOs) also launched campaigns, seeking to persuade the major food industry players to pledge to source only cage-free eggs. Many companies, grocery stores, and restaurants were developing or modifying their policies on this issue. Some organizations announced that they aimed to go cage-free in their egg supply by 2025.[20]

Mathers had read an article that explained that California had passed legislation mandating that each hen have one square foot of space, or 144 square inches, in the cages.[21] Mathers had seen pictures of the conventional or caged housing system (again refer to **Exhibit 2, Figure 1**). Mathers looked over the picture of the hens in these conventional or battery cages. "We certainly can do better than this," he said after looking at all those hens crowded into cages. "But there are other considerations as well," thought Mathers. "What impact does cage-free housing have on food safety? Food safety was paramount in IFRC's materiality chart. What does it mean to worker welfare, and how will it impact our other sustainability goals? Was enriched caged colony production a reasonable alternative?"

MATHERS CONTINUES HIS RESEARCH

While Mathers understood from the activists' position that sourcing only cage-free eggs seemed like a reasonable way to improve animal welfare, IFRC's existing suppliers revealed several serious dilemmas. First, there were not enough cage-free eggs in the supply chain to meet consumer demand if the entire food industry transitioned to cage-free. Conversion to cage-free housing would take years and required significant capital investment and additional acreage on which to build the facilities.[22] The overall number of birds in the system would need to increase in order to deliver the same output as the current egg supply. This was because cage-free hens had a 25% higher mortality rate, due to the natural pecking habits and cannibalism of hens. That increase had implications on sustainability, from growing more grain (with concomitant water and fertilizer needs), to transporting the incremental feed and chickens, and the production of more manure. These demands to convert were coming on the heels of a recent outbreak of highly pathogenic Avian Influenza that resulted in the record death of 50.4 million birds (out of 300 million birds, including chickens, turkeys, and hens) in 639 flocks, in 46 states. This pushed the egg supply way below the 5-year average of supply.[23]

Continuing his research, Mathers learned that in 2015 the Coalition for a Sustainable Egg Supply undertook a research project, seeking to answer the question, "What is the best way to produce eggs?"[24] The Laying Hen Housing Research Project studied three of the four basic systems (conventional caged, enriched caged colony, and cage-free). Free-range and pasture-raised cage-free systems were not studied.

Animal Health

Insofar as animal health and well-being were concerned, physiological data from the Laying Hen Housing Research Project did not spot any acute or chronic stress for hens in any of the three housing system.[25] Mathers had read that cage-free (also known as free-run aviary) systems had the highest hen mortality rate, compared to conventional or caged housing and enriched caged colonies. The hen mortality rate in conventional or caged housing was the lowest of the three systems, 4.8% in conventional caged, 5.2% in enriched colony caged, and 11.7% in cage-free. "That means it would take more hens to produce the same number of eggs. More hens mean more feed, more grain, more irrigation and water, more fertilizer to grow the grain, and more costs to harvest and transport the grain," Mathers concluded. Feed cost represented about 60% of the cost eggs production.[26] It was also harder for those working in these systems to find dead birds in the enriched and cage-free housing system. One supplier told Mathers that the more hens can roam, the less able the producer is to control the quality of feed and what the hens consume, including fecal matter and carcasses of dead hens.

Food Safety

Study results on the safety of the eggs revealed that there was no difference in incidences of Salmonella in eggshells among the housing systems. There was no measured difference in the quality of the eggs two days after they were laid, and anyway, any nutritional difference among egg types would have to be stated on the egg carton.[27] One study asserted that there were no differences in the eggs' nutritional value in the three systems.[28] However, multiple studies had conflicting results. One study was conducted by the *Journal of Food Control*, examining bacteria levels on eggs in the various housing systems. That study did find measurable difference between caged and cage-free eggs, with greater microbiological contamination on the eggshell surface from cage-free eggs.[29]

Environmental Impact

Mathers also researched the environmental impact of the three systems. Energy use and costs were similar among the three systems, in the controlled laboratory experiment.[30] Indoor air quality was poorest in cage-free systems. Ammonia and particulate matter were highest there, as manure was not removed as readily as with conveyor systems that were removing feces in caged environments; there was also more dust in the air.

He noted that the egg industry prided itself on reducing the environmental impact over the last 50 years in egg production. However, significant environment hurdles remained: efficiency in feed production, least-environmental cost feed sourcing, and bird manure management (raising more hens meant producing more manure), the last resulting in greenhouse gas emissions.[31]

Affordability

As far as food affordability was studied, the research revealed that the average operating and capital costs to produce a dozen eggs were as follows: conventional caged was 67¢. The comparable cost for the enriched colony caged was 75.6¢ and cage-free systems costs were 91.3¢. These costs included feed, hens, labor, energy, and capital costs.

Mathers knew the IFRC sold eggs from the array of egg-production systems. He checked the prices of these systems of a dozen eggs at one of the IFRC member stores. One dozen conventional (or caged or battery) eggs retailed for $1.49 – 3.49; enriched colony egg prices were $3.49 – $4.79; cage-free or free-run aviary eggs were about $3.29 - $6.49, and free-range or pasture-raised eggs sold between $6.19 and $8.99. Mathers knew that for shoppers who came into the stores, eggs were in the top ten of items in a consumer's shopping basket. For online shoppers, over a third of them had eggs as a purchased item. "Besides the conventional eggs, we've been selling cage-free eggs in our stores for more than a decade," Mathers noted as he reviewed the recent sales data from the dairy department. Only about 25% of all eggs sold were free-range eggs and this had remained steady for the previous five or so years. Mathers concluded that the price of eggs mattered to the average IFRC customer.

The issue of affordability was a concern for IFRC members and the customers they served. The price of a dozen eggs – a household staple and low-cost but important protein source – would rise with cage-free production. For many households on fixed or low incomes, the conventional egg was a low-cost dietary staple. Mathers was mindful of the food deserts where its member-stores operated. "How do we improve the welfare of animals in our food production system while retaining our commitment to keeping food affordable?" wondered Mathers.

Worker Health and Safety

Mathers examined the research on the safety of workers who harvested eggs in the different environments. Workers' exposure to airborne particles and toxins (such as ammonia or bacteria) was measured and their bending and other movement to gather eggs was also studied. The Coalition study evaluated no discernable differences in three environments.[32] However, other publications contended that workers who had to harvest eggs in cage-free housing systems were exposed to poorer air quality because of the random placement of bird litter and because hens scratched up the dust.[33] A

2020 research article reported that the number of labor hours needed to harvest eggs was inversely proportional to the density of the housing production system. Statedly differently, the labor cost per dozen eggs was lowest in caged environments, higher in enriched colonies, and highest in cage-free environments.[34]

Mathers' final step in his research was to call suppliers. He first called industry expert and President of the National Association of Egg Farmers, Ken Klippen. Klippen had 40 years of experience in the poultry industry, with several important and high-level assignments in the field. Klippen explained the following to Mathers.

> The chickens' welfare should be centered on scientific principles. When comparing eggs produced in the three different production systems (conventional, enriched, and cage-free pasture-raised), all things considered, the caged layer system is the best from the standpoint of the chicken, food safety, worker safety, climate protection, and protecting against the spread of highly pathogenic Avian Influenza.

Another supplier told Mathers that typically those harvesting eggs come from all sources of categories of workers. These sources include migrants, and the degree to which these workers hadworking papers or could work legally was hard to know. The jobs were low-paying.

Mathers organized all his information into a chart, condensing the materials from the Research Project and his other readings.[35] (**See Case Exhibit 3.**) Mathers did one final check to see if the Humane Society or similar groups presented any research, refuting the research he had found on the different egg production systems. He could not, not even among those countering the affordability or mortality research.

TIME TO MAKE THE RECOMMENDATION

Mathers owed the board information on his research of egg-producing systems. He also was expected to recommend whether IFRC should make a public pledge on sourcing eggs solely from cage-free hens. He asked himself the following questions:

> The activists demand a pledge not to sell anything but cage-free eggs by 2025. Is there some middle ground? Are there other egg production processes that might be more amenable to the activists? Should I prioritize affordability for customers over animal rights? How do I incorporate IFRC's different policy statements and our materiality assessment? Which stakeholders and their interests matter most to IFRC? Once I figure out who or what is most important to IFRC, can I better defend my recommendation?

Exhibit 1: IFRC's Financial Materiality Assessment Chart

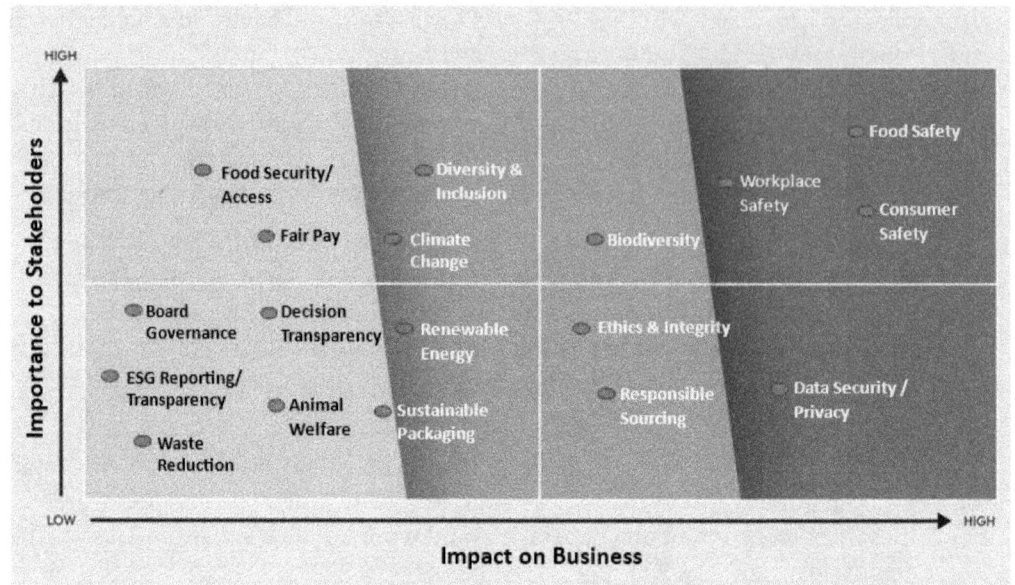

The materiality assessment represents stakeholder sentiment at a moment in time. Current events, changes in public opinion and other exogenous factors can easily change how stakeholders prioritize issues of concern and how those issues impact the demands on the business and how operates.

Source: IFRC Internal Document

Exhibit 2: Photographs of Egg Production Systems

Figure 1: Conventional or Caged or Battery Production Systems[36]

Figure 1 Source: https://zootecnicainternational.com/featured/housing-systems-laying-hen-husbandry/

Figure 2: Enriched Caged Colony Production System[37]

Figure 2 Source: https://www.bigdutchman.com/en/egg-production/news/photos/aviary-systems/

Exhibit 2: Photographs of Egg Production Systems (Cont'd)

Figure 3: Cage-Free or Free-Run Aviary Production System

Figure 3 Source: https://www.bigdutchman.com/en/egg-production/news/photos/aviary-systems/

Exhibit 3: Mathers' Chart on Egg Production Systems

Factor Studied	Conventional or Caged or Battery Production	Enriched Caged Colony Production	Cage-Free or Free-Run Aviary Production
Animal Health Foot	Highest number of foot problems but not severe as cage-free	Intermediate range of problems and their severity	Lowest number of foot injuries but most severe foot problems
Animal Health Keel*	Lowest keel injury	Intermediate injury	Highest keel injury
Hen Mortality Percent**	4.7 %	5.1%	11.6%
Food Safety	No difference	No difference	No difference
Environmental Impact***	Equal air quality between this system and enriched production system Same impact on energy usage	About ½ of the ammonia emissions compared to cage-free Same impact on energy usage	8 to 10 times higher in ammonia and particulate compared to the other two production systems Same impact on energy usage
Worker Health	Low toxins Irritated eyes; itchy rash	Same low toxins Nasal irritation, mucous/ phlegm	Highest toxins; most ergonomically challenged; respiratory health was marginally worse for laborers in this environment, even with masks Nasal irritation, throat irritation, cough, mucous/phlegm, shortness of breath, itchy rash
Risk of Avian Influenza****	Best at containment	The more the hens can roam, the greater the spread	Most contagious and can easily infect an entire flock
Cost per dozen eggs	67 cents	75.6 cents	91.3 cents

*Keel health refers to the degree to which the breastbone is attached to the wings of the hen.

**Hens naturally have pecking orders in flocks and peck each other to death. There are also more diseases. Hens have an average life span of 18-24 months in any production system.

***Particulate arises from hens scratching the ground. More flying raises dust particles in the air. Fecal matter is scattered throughout the cage-free system.

****Avian influenza (AI) is caused by an influenza Type A virus which can infect poultry and is often fatal. It can spread from migratory waterfowl to commercial flocks. Multiple severe outbreaks have occurred in the US and globally, including ones in 2014-2015, 2017, and 2022.

NOTES

[1] This case is disguised. Both the names of the firm and the protagonist have been changed. The case is based on an actual situation with a real organization.

[2] This is drawn from the organization's archives and a book it published in 2010 about the organization's formation.

[3] Davis, D. (2017, June 16.). Amazon solidifies its hold on affluent shoppers with purchase of Whole Foods. Retrieved from www.digitalcommerce.com: https://www.digitalcommerce.com.

[4] Rhone, A., VerPloeg, M., Dicken, C., Williams, R., & Breneman, V. (2017). Low-income and low supermarket-access census tracts, 2010-2015. Washington, DC: U.S. Department of Agriculture.

[5] Inouye, J. (2021). Double and dynamic materiality: Key drivers for business sustainability and success. London: Wolters Kluwer.

[6] Aronson, D., Friend, G., & Winston, A. (2018, October 13). Materiality is broken. But it doesn't have to be. Retrieved from www.sustainabilitybrands.com: https://sustainablebrands.com; NYU Stern Center for Sustainable Business. (2019). Sustainability Materiality Matrices Explained. New York: NYU Stern Center for Sustainable Business; Calace, D. (2020, September 2). Double and dynamic: Understanding the changing perspectives on materiality. Retrieved from www.sasb.org: https://www.sasb.org.

[7] Garst, J., Maas, K., & Suijs, J. (September 22 2022). Materiality is an art, not a science: Selecting ESG topics for sustainability reports. California Management Review.

[8] U. S. Department of Agriculture. (2023, July 22). Poultry and eggs. Retrieved from www.ers.usda.gov/topics/animal-products/poultry-eggs/

[9] Dunham, J. and Associates. (2018). U.S. egg impact report. United Egg Producers; Dunham, J. and Associates. (2020). U.S. egg impact report. United Egg Producers.

[10] United Egg Producers. (2021). Facts-Stats. https://unitedegg.com: United Egg Producers.

[11] Coalition for Sustainable Egg Supply. (2015). Laying Hen Housing Research Project; Good, K. (n.d.). Think you know 'free range' and 'cage free' Chicken? Think Again. Retrieved from One Green Planet: http://www.onegreenplanet.org.; Zhao, Y., Shepherd, T., Swanson, J., Mench, J., Karcher, D., & Xin, H. (March, 2015). Comparative evaluation of three egg prductions systems: Housing characteristics and management practices. Poultry Science, 475-84.

[12] United Egg Producers. (n.d. (b)). Evolution of U.S. egg farming. Retrieved from unitedegg.com: https://unitedegg.com.

[13] United Egg Producers. (n.d. (a)). Terms. https://unitedegg.com-terms: United Egg Producers.

[14] Bjork, T. (2019, June 6). Conventional or cage-free eggs: It's about choice. Retrieved from Iowa Farm Bureau: https://iowafarmbureau.com.

[15] The Humane Society. (n.d.). Cage-free vs. battery-cage eggs. Retrieved from The Humane Society of the U.S.: https://humanesociety.org.

[16] Conway, A. (2018, October 17). How to protect poultry operations from animal activists. Retrieved from www.wattegnet.com: www.wattagnet.com.

[17] U.S. Department of Agriculture. (2016). Grademarked Product Label Submission Checklist. Washington, D.C.: U.S. Department of Agriculture.

[18] Bjork, T. (2019, June 6). Conventional or cage-free eggs: It's about choice. Retrieved from Iowa Farm Bureau: https://iowafarmbureau.com.; The Humane Society. (n.d.). Cage-free vs. battery-cage eggs. Retrieved from The Humane Society of the U.S.: https://humanesociety.org.

[19] Mintus, C. (2021, June 17). More states in the U.S. to switch to cage-free eggs. Retrieved from The Poultry Site: https://www.thepoultrysite.com; Block, K. (2021, December 22). Breaking: Massachusetts passes law to end cruel, immobilizing cages for egg-laying hens. Retrieved from Blog-Humane Society: https://blog.humanesociety.org.

[20] Mintus, C. (2021, June 17). More states in the U.S. to switch to cage-free eggs. Retrieved from The Poultry Site: https://www.thepoultrysite.com.

[21] Mintus, C. (2021, June 17). More states in the U.S. to switch to cage-free eggs. Retrieved from The Poultry Site: https://www.thepoultrysite.com.; The Humane Society. (n.d.). Cage-free vs. battery-cage eggs. Retrieved from The Humane Society of the U.S.: https://humanesociety.org.

[22] Casey, C. (2023, February 28). Why cage-free eggs could be on shaky ground. Retrieved from www.fooddive.com: https://www.fooddive.com/news/why-cage-free-eggs-could-be-on-shaky-ground.

[23] (US Department of Agriculture, 2022)

[24] Coalition for Sustainable Egg Supply. (2015). Laying Hen Housing Research Project.

[25] Ibid.

[26] Mintus, C. (2021, June 17). More states in the U.S. to switch to cage-free eggs. Retrieved from The Poultry Site: https://www.thepoultrysite.com.

[27] Best Food Facts. (2019, August 16). What's the difference between cage-free and regular eggs? Retrieved from Best Food Facts: https://www.bestfoodfacts.org.

[28] Best Food Facts. (2019, August 16). What's the difference between cage-free and regular eggs? Retrieved from Best Food Facts: https://www.bestfoodfacts.org.

[29] Parisi, M.A., Northcutt, J.K., Smith, D.P., Steinberg, E.L., Dawson, P.L. (2014). "Microbiological contamination of shell eggs produced in conventional and free-range housing systems," Food Control, pp. 161-65.

[30] Coalition for Sustainable Egg Supply. (2015). Laying Hen Housing Research Project.

[31] Xin, H., Ibarburu, M., Vold, L., & Pelletier, N. (2013). A comparative assessment of the environmental footprint of the U.S. Egg Industry in 1960 and 2010. Egg Industry Center Iowa State University.

[32] Coalition for Sustainable Egg Supply. (2015). Laying Hen Housing Research Project.

[33] Bjork, T. (2019, June 6). Conventional or cage-free eggs: It's about choice. Retrieved from Iowa Farm Bureau: https://iowafarmbureau.com

[34] Brannan, K., & Anderson, K. (March 2021). Examination of the impact of range, cage-free, modified systems, and conventional cage environments on the labor inputs committed to bird care for three brown egg layer strains. Journal of Applied Poultry Research.

[35] Coalition for Sustainable Egg Supply. (2015). Laying Hen Housing Research Project.

[36] Windhorst, H. (2017, July 4). Housing systems in laying hens husbandry: First part. Retrieved from www.zootecnicalinternational.com: https://zootecnicalinternational.com

[37] Egg Farmers of Canada. (2016, August 16). The 5 things you find in enriched colony housing. Retrieved from www.eggfarmers.ca: https://www.eggfarmers.ca.

Can Hens Save Dodiya Farms?

Kinjal Jethwani, LJ Institute of Management Studies
Kumar Ramchandani, LJ Institute of Management Studies

Midnight, May 20, 2021: Under a cloudless sky in Bantwa village, Junagadh district, Gujarat, India, Ranjit Dodiya started up the irrigation system to water his 50 acre farm. He reflected on the challenges of the past three years. In 2018 heavy rainfall ruined most of the harvest. In 2019, drought reduced the yield, and a 2020 locust[1] attack had destroyed the standing crop in minutes. These calamities caused three consecutive unprofitable years. Now, Dodiya considered whether to launch an egg-producing poultry business on one acre of his farm. He thought this idea might offer an opportunity to earn a profit (or at least lose less money) in years when bad weather or pests hurt his crops; yet, he also saw potential operational and financial risks in this idea.

He needed to decide: Should Dodiya Farms develop an egg-laying operation? If not, what else might he do to save his farm?

A SON FOLLOWS IN HIS FATHER'S FOOTSTEPS AT DODIYA FARMS

Dodiya Farms was started in 1987 by Ranjit Dodiya's father, Ranmal Dodiya. Ranjit Dodiya admired his father's early decision to invest in modern techniques and agricultural tools and equipment(making it possible for Dodiya to rent this machinery to other farmers). Even in 2021, only a few other farms in the region owned two threshers.

Dodiya's father believed in the idea of *"learning by doing; do every task on your own, so that you don't need to depend on others."* From the age of seven, Ranjit Dodiya helped after school with tasks such as removing weeds, harvesting crops, and caring for cattle. At age eleven he learned how to plow with cattle, and by age thirteen he could drive a tractor. His father taught him how to analyze soil chemistry, acquire high-quality seeds, apply fertilizers and pesticides, irrigate, select which crops to grow each season, when to sow, and how to prevent (or cope with) environmental challenges and pests. He also emphasized the value of a good education.

In 1996 a heart attack killed Ranmal Dodiya. As his only son, Ranjit Dodiya took charge at age fourteen, and was the youngest farmer in Bantwa at that time. By then he knew how to carry out every task on the farm. He was thankful that his father prepared him so well. And, inspired by his father's advice, by age 23 Dodiya completed a Master in Commerce (M.Com.) degree.

Like most Indian farmers, Dodiya carefully planned around the likely onset of monsoon season. Kharif (summer/monsoon) crops like rice, maize, soybean, or cotton were planted in the June-August Southwest monsoon season. Winter crops (grown November–March) included cereals (e.g., wheat, barley, oats), pulses (e.g., chickpeas), and oilseeds (e.g., linseed, mustard.[2]

Many farmers sourced their water from the Bantwa dam reservoir. Since this dam was not connected to a natural water flow or river, a weak monsoon could severely reduce the water supply. Some farms (including Dodiya Farm) invested in irrigation systems. Scheduled power outages, planned by the state government to ration power, as well as unscheduled outages, sometimes delayed irrigation and other farming tasks that required electricity.

Consistent with his father's legacy of agricultural innovation, Ranjit Dodiya rotated crops to keep his soil healthy. One year he grew groundnut (a short-duration summer crop) and wheat (a short-duration winter crop). The next year he grew cotton (a long-duration summer crop). In 2021, and nearing age 40, Dodiya was proud of his farm, and believed its yield was 10% to 15% higher than farms that did not rotate crops.

Still, the 2018 floods, 2019 drought and 2020 locust attack hurt the farm badly. In most years Dodiya borrowed money in the form of short-term working capital loans, but in the three most recent 'tough' years he dug into his own savings to pay the interest on those loans.

Crop infections (fungus, bacteria, and worms) remained an ever-present threat. Pink-ball worms threatened cotton crops and were dangerous to handle. If an appropriate pesticide was not applied in the first growing stage, the entire cotton crop might be lost. Even a one-week delay in treatment could reduce the yield. Meanwhile, new germ mutations necessitated expensive new treatments.

Realizing no farmer was lucky every year, Dodiya considered alternative sources of income that might help offset future losses from droughts, floods, pests, and diseases. A childhood friend, Mahesh Patel, recommended that he set up an egg-laying business(as Patel himself had, in 2019). He told Dodiya that his own operation was performing well, but added a note of caution: "One needs to keep a constant watch on feed cost," since chick feed constituted 70% to 80% of total egg-laying operational costs.[3] .Intrigued by Patel's positive experience, Dodiya set out to learn more.

POULTRY EGG PRODUCTION INDUSTRY OVERVIEW

Meat production and egg production were the two forms of poultry farming. Egg production ranged from small backyard operations to large, integrated egg-laying operations. A backyard operation entailed raising a few hens at a time to supply a family with eggs for their own use, and excess eggs might be sold locally. Integrated egg production operations housed hens in temperature-controlled buildings, fed them specially formulated feed, and mechanized some tasks. Many households had a few chickens and some farms raised a greater number of hens for sale at regional markets, but far fewer integrated egg production operations existed in India. Dodiya learned that India's chicken-raising and egg laying costs were among the lowest in the world.

The $25.4 billion poultry market (in 2018) was projected to reach $ 63.1 billion by 2024.[4] In 2019 world egg production reached 83 million tonnes (2,200 pounds per tonne).[5] a 63% increase from levels in 2000.Asia produced 62% of the world's eggs, followed by the Americas (21%), Europe (13%), and Africa (4%).[6] China produced the most eggs (35% of total) followed by the United States of America (8%), and India (7%).[7]

India and China were the largest consumer markets in the world, with 2020 populations of almost 1.4 billion each. Average annual egg consumption per person more than doubled between 2014 and 2019, from 30 to 68. One survey revealed that in Gujarat, consumption of eggs increased by 50% in the previous two decades.[8]

INTEGRATED EGG LAYING OPERATIONS

Day-old chicks were purchased from local hatcheries. Through three stages of growth, batches of chicks were shifted from smaller to larger cages as they grew larger and hungrier (**Exhibit 1**):

- Brooder Phase (first 8 weeks): Chicks could not yet lay eggs.
- Grower Phase (9-16 weeks): Chicks grew quickly and needed a lot of feed. It was important to properly manage Growers, since their reproductive organs developed during this period, and this could affect their egg production capacity in the following phase..
- Layer Phase (17-72 weeks): Laying hens required the most feed.

When a cohort of birds moved up to larger cages, their prior cages were emptied, cleaned, sanitized, and left empty for the subsequent four weeks (**Exhibit 2**).

Factors that could affect egg production included climate, breed of hen, the laying house design, lighting schedule, feed quantity and quality, and how and when eggs were collected.[9] A major risk was the highly contagious avian flu (bird flu). If detected in just one bird on a farm it was necessary to destroy an entire flock to ensure that flu was fully eradicated there. After an infection, the farm would have to be deep-cleaned, and egg-laying sheds might be required to sit empty for six months.

On average in India, wholesale egg prices (Rupees, or Rs, per 100 eggs)[10] were 335 (2015), 391 (2016), 382 (2017), 400 (2018), 414 (2019), and 428 (2020).[11] In 2020, wholesale prices ranged from Rs 323 to Rs 548.[12] International Egg Commission (IEC) chairman Suresh Chitturi noted that Indian egg prices had reached record highs. Egg consumption in India in 2021 was low compared to many countries, at 77 eggs per person per year, but was expected to rise to 154 per person within five years.[13]

Other than sales of eggs, egg-laying operations generated other revenues as well:

- Unproductive hens, such as those older than 72 weeks, were sold for soup or other purposes. Layer bird prices, at about Rs 54 per bird[14] were about 60% lower than prices for chickens raised for their meat.
- Poultry litter could be sold or used as organic fertilizer.[15]
- Poultry feed gunny bags could also be sold, but at very low prices.

Prices of day-old chicks, previously Rs 30-40 rose 50% to Rs 50-60 in 2020.[16] Maize and soya together comprised 90% of the total poultry feed ingredients.[17] A sharp increase in soya meal cost (82%) caused this rapid price increase.

LEARNING MORE ABOUT EGG LAYING OPERATIONS

In March 2021, Dodiya visited Mahesh Patel's poultry farm to observe its operations, from purchasing and growing day-old chicks to gathering and selling hens' eggs. Patel suggested he also visit Junagadh Agricultural University (JAU)[18] to learn about subsidies provided by the state and central government. In an interactive seminar there, Dodiya learned about the machinery required, government schemes, loan facilities, subsidies, the market for eggs, export possibilities, and technology and human resource requirements. JAU instructors reported that in a hot and humid climate a commercial hen might produce180 to 200 eggs per year, whereas in a more temperate climate she might produce 250 to 300 eggs per year. An instructor noted that in Gujarat, "where the summer temperature varies between 25⁰C and 45⁰C, while winter temperature ranges between 15⁰C and 35⁰C degrees," egg-laying farms produced at the high end of that range.

Another JAU expert, discussing the risk of bird flu, said regular check-ups of chicks and the use of vaccines and medicines were important to a successful egg-laying operation, and that it was also advisable to purchase special-purpose bird insurance. The expert referred participants to a *Poultry Layer Farming* report, which helped Dodiya consider financial issues.

He planned to allocate one acre of farmland to the egg-laying operation. The cost to level this land was estimated at Rs 250,000. He would need to build a shed and housing for four workers and would also have to purchase cages and other equipment. Although Dodiya had never obtained a term loan to purchase items like these, he believed he could get a Rs 3,000,000 term loan and also might be eligible for government interest subsidies to help pay to improve and equip the property for a laying operation.

To finance day-to-day operating expenses, Dodiya planned to obtain a working capital loan of Rs 3,500,000. Still, his investigation revealed he would likely need to spend about Rs 2,040,000 of his own money to launch the egg-laying operation. His expected total financing was (see also **Exhibit 3**):

> To acquire fixed assets:
> > Rs 3,000,000 term loan
> > Rs 1,107,000 personal contribution by Ranjit Dodiya
> > Rs 4,107,000 fixed assets investment

> Annual operating expenses of Rs 4,713,000 funded by:
> > Rs 3,500,000 working capital loan
> > Rs   931,000 personal contribution by Ranjit Dodiya
> > Rs 4,431,000 annual operating expenses

> Total   **Rs 8,538,000**financing needed for Year One (4,107,000 + 4,431,000)

Both the term loan and working capital loan charged an annual interest rate of 12%. The term loan was to be repaid in six equal annual installments (interest and principal).The working capital loan could be repaid at the discretion of the borrower, but had to be repaid in full by the end of the sixth year. All farmers were eligible for government-issued 6% interest subsidies on working capital loans, and farmers were not required to pay an income tax.

Unsure as to an appropriate discount rate for evaluating a potential egg-laying operation, Dodiya reached out to some JAU instructors and his own financial advisor, a chartered accountant). Based on their guidance and the model project report, he decided on a 15% discount rate. Next, he set out to evaluate a baseline case (expected costs and revenues), and worst and best cases. He was concerned that feed cost could rise sharply; and knew that per-hen yearly egg production was a key revenue driver (**Exhibit 4**).

Now Ranjit Dodiya needed to decide: was egg laying a viable business? How soon could Dodiya Farms expect to recover its initial investment? What if actual revenues from this operation were lower than he expected? What if operating expenses were higher than he expected? Would egg laying income be sufficient to service the necessary loans?

Exhibit 1: Brooder, Grower, and Layer Sheds

Batch	1+1+5 Cage System of Poultry Farming						
	Brooder Shed Weeks	Grower Shed Weeks	Layer Shed 1 Weeks	Layer Shed 2 Weeks	Layer Shed 3 Weeks	Layer Shed 4 Weeks	Layer Shed 5 Weeks
1	0-8	9-16	17-72*	-	-	-	-
2	13-20	21-28	-	29-85	-	-	-
3	25-32	33-40	-	-	41-97	-	-
4	37-44	45-52	-	-	-	53-109	-
5	49-56	57-64	-	-	-	-	65-121
One Year = 52 weeks.							
* Most layers became unproductive by week 72 and were culled.							
Source: Ranjit Dodiya, based on advice given by Mr. Mahesh Patel and the JAU workshop.							

Exhibit 2: Bird Flow Chart

	Year 1	Year 2	Year 3	Year 4	Year 5	Year 6
1. Number of batches purchased	4	4	4	5	4	4
2. Number of brooder weeks	28	36	32	36	36	32
3. Number of grower weeks	24	32	36	36	32	36
4. Number of layer weeks	36	216	244	240	244	244
5. Number of batches culled	0	2	5	4	4	5
Assumption: On a calendar-year basis, Batch 1 arrived the 13th week of year 1.						
Source: Data provided by Ranjit Dodiya based on inputs given by Mahesh Patel and the JAU workshop instructor.						

Exhibit 2 summarizes how day-old chicks were assigned to brooder shed batches (for 8 weeks), then moved to the grower shed (for 8 weeks) and subsequently to a layer shed (for 56 weeks).

At age 72 weeks (Week 32 of year 2), that batch was culled (no batch needed to be culled in year 1).

When a batch of chicks moved to a bigger cage, their previous cage remained empty for four weeks, to help prevent undetected disease from spreading to new chicks.

Exhibit 3: Fixed Assets and Operational Costs for Proposed Egg-Laying Operation

	Rs Per Unit	Rs Total (000)
I. Fixed Assets to be Acquired		
a. Land Development		250
b. Shed & Building		
Construct brooder cum grower shed (2500 Sq. ft.)	320	800
Construct layer sheds (under cage system) (5000 Sq. ft.)	320	1600
Storeroom for Eggs and Storeroom for Feed (300 Sq. ft.)	320	96
Office Building (200 Sq. ft.)	350	70
Office Furniture Computer/ Printer		125
Generator Room (100 Sq. ft.)	320	32
Workers Quarters (4 workers) (200 Sq. ft.)	200	40
c. Cages & Equipment		
Laying house (6250 cages)	75	470
Other equipment (packaging, manure handling)		200
Water system (bore well, I HP Electric motor pump set, water tank, pipeline)		225
Electrification/ Sprinkler/ Refrigeration/ Heating System		200
Total Fixed Assets (a+b+c)		**4107**
II. Operational Costs		
Cost of day old Chicks (10,000 birds)	50	500
Feed Cost		2561
Medicine, vaccine, labour and miscellaneous charges		60
Insurance cost per bird	4	40
Other Expenses		1270
Total Operational Costs		**4431**
Total Cash Outlay (I+II)		**8537**
Discount Rate/ Cost of Capital 15% for calculation purpose as reported by Ranjit Dodiya		
Assume negligible or zero scrap value of machinery at end of Year 6		
Source: Data provided by Ranjit Dodiya based on inputs given by Mr. Mahesh Patel and workshop at JAU		

Exhibit 4: Egg-Laying Operations: Base Case, Worst Case, Best Case

Assumptions based on stage	Brooder	Grower	Layer
Mortality during normal 72 week life span	2%	3%	5%
Birds availability	2625	2575	2500
Feed Consumption per hen per week (kg)	0.20	0.40	0.70
Manure Output (kg per week per bird)	0.30	0.30	0.50
Cost of Medicine per Bird per Week (Rs)	0.30	0.25	0.25
Assumptions for Worst, Base, Best cases	**Worst Case**	**Base Case**	**Best case**
Eggs production per hen (annual)	200	250	300
Eggs production per hen (week)	3.80	4.80	5.77
Feed cost per Kg (Rs)	35	25	18

Other Assumptions

Cost of day-old chicks (DOC) (Rs)	50
Numbers of chicks per Batch	2500
Additional Birds from supplier free of cost (5% of Batch considering mortality rate	125
Number of Birds available for Culling	2375
Price per sellable culled bird (Rs)	54
Insurance per bird (Rs) (Provides indemnity against death of bird, but not for any consequential loss or loss of production/ sale)	4
Selling price per Egg for Year 1,2, 3 (Rs)	5.00
Selling price per Egg for Year 4,5, 6 (Rs)	6.00
Wages 1 Manager: Rs 200,000, 4 labourers: Rs 400,000	600,000
Power and fuel (average annualized) (Rs)	600,000
Property insurance (average annualized) (Rs)	10,000
Feed in one gunny bag (kg)	75
Selling price of gunny bag (Rs)	25
Selling price of 1 kg or manure	2
Misc Expenses	60,000
Bank interest for Rs 3M Term Loan	12%
Annual number of Payments for Rs 3M Term Loan	6
Bank interest for Rs 3.5M Working Capital Loan (principle to be repaid by end of Year 6)	12%
Government Working Capital Loan Subsidy percent	6%
See Note 2 re Deferred Payment of Working Capital Loan (to be fully repaid in Year 6)	
Project Life (for purposes of ROI analysis)	6 years
NOTES	
1. In India, farm income was exempted from income tax.	
2. Ranjit Dodiya decided to repay the working capital loan in the following manner:Rs. 0.58M each in first five years and remaining Rs. 0.6M in sixth year.	
Source: Ranjit Dodiya, based on information from Mahesh Patel and JAU	

NOTES

[1] Locusts, a species of short-horned grasshopper, can form dense, highly mobile swarms that feed on trees and crops. "About locusts," November 04, 2019. https://www.agriculture.gov.au/pests-diseases-weeds/locusts/about/aboutlocusts

[2] Srija, A. (1996). Cropping Seasons of India- Kharif & Rabi. Retrieved from http://www.arthapedia.in/: http://www.arthapedia.in/index.php%3Ftitle=CroppingseasonsofIndia-Kharif%2526Rabi

[3] Mallick, P. M. (2020). Broiler Poultry Feed Cost Optimization Using Linear Programming Technique. . Journal of Operations and Strategic Planning , 3(1), 31–57.

[4] FAO. (2021). World Food and Agriculture – Statistical Yearbook 2021. Rome. . Retrieved from https://doi.org/10.4060/cb4477en: https://www.fao.org/3/cb4477en/cb4477en.pdf

[5] Ibid

[6] Ibid

[7] Ibid

[8] Rupera, H. K. (2021, March 15). times of india. State's milk, egg production highest in 15 yrs , pp. https://timesofindia.indiatimes.com/city/ahmedabad/states-milk-egg-production-highest-in-15-yrs/articleshow/81500168.cms

[9] FAO. (2003, FAO (Food and Agricultural Organization of the United Nations). 2003. Chapter 1: Egg production:https://www.fao.org/3/y4628e/y4628e03.htm#TopOfPage 150. Rome, Italy, 2003. https://www). A Guide for the Production and Sale of Eggs. Food Agricultural Bulletin. Retrieved from Food and Agricultural Organization of the United Nations https://www.fao.org/: https://www.fao.org/3/y4628e/y4628e03.htm#TopOfPage

[10] On May 2021 1USD was equal to Rs.73

[11] NECC. (n.d.). NECC (Indian National Egg Coordination Committee). Daily/ Monthly Egg Prices. Retrieved from https://www.e2necc.com/: https://www.e2necc.com/home/eggprice

[12] Ibid

[13] Clements, M. (2021, February 17). India's egg producers looking to a positive future. Retrieved from wattagnet.com: Clements, M. 2021, "India's egg producers looking to a positive future", wattagnet.com, Feb 17, 2021. https://www.wattagnet.com/egg/egg-production/article/15532975/indias-egg-producers-looking-to-a-positive-future

[14] PoultryBazaar. (2022, August). Layer Rates. Retrieved August 5, 2022, from https://www.poultrybazaar.net/: Poultry Bazaar. 2022, Layer Rates.https://www.poultrybazaar.net/monthly-rate-sheet/Layer-Rates/, accessed on August 05, 2022. (both updated prices and historical prices available on this ink)

[15] Hamilton, E. (2021, May 03). The surprising power of chicken manure. Agronomy , pp. https://www.agronomy.org/news/science-news/surprising-power-chicken-manure/.

[16] Ghosal, S. (2021, April 08). Poultry prices up by more than 50% in a year as animal feed drives up costs. Economic Times , pp. Ghosal, S. 2021. Phttps://economictimes.indiatimes.com/news/economy/agriculture/poultry-prices-up-by-more-than-50-in-a-year-as-animal-feed-drives-up- cost.

[17] Amit. (2020, October 04). Indian poultry industry:- Challenges, problems and opportunities. . Retrieved from https://thepoultrypunch.com/: https://thepoultrypunch.com/2020/10/indian-poultry-industry-challenges-problems-and-opportunities/

[18] Junagadh Agricultural University (JAU), in Junagadh, Gujarat, offers higher education in Agriculture, Agricultural Engineering & Technology, Fisheries Science, Veterinary & Animal Husbandry, and Horticulture. http://www.jau.in/

Columbia Green Technologies (A): Scaling in the Green Roof Market

NACRA
NORTH AMERICAN CASE
RESEARCH ASSOCIATION

Charla Mathwick, Portland State University

Vanessa Keitges stepped into the role of CEO at Columbia Green Technologies (CGT) in 2010, growing it to become the dominant green infrastructure and green roof materials supplier on the West Coast. The Portland, Oregon-based company initially launched with green roofing systems that harnessed nature-based technologies to mitigate the damage caused by stormwater runoff. Having installed 2,500 roof gardens by 2022, Keitges could see that demand had accelerated, as extreme weather events increasingly overwhelmed stormwater infrastructure across the U.S. With a 16.2% CAGR and a forecasted global investment opportunity surpassing $5.37 billion by 2030,[1] the green roof industry had finally reached its inflection point.[2]

Although Keitges had successfully raised venture capital when CGT was an early-stage startup, she knew that securing funding to scale her business at a rate comparable to the expanding market would be an uphill battle. Female entrepreneurs had received only 1.9% of all venture capital in 2022.[3] Consequently, the pressure was on her executive team to build a compelling case for investment in their firm's North American expansion.

With less than a month to gear up for the first of several meetings during Q1 2023, Keitges and her team had begun to prepare for a Series C funding round to finance a scalable rollout of the organization. The preliminary plan was to increase the sales force from three to twelve field reps and to position them in the highest growth markets. However, the immediate decision facing the team involved choosing which markets to target. They needed an approach for prioritizing where demand for green infrastructure and green roofing solutions was most likely to take off geographically.

GREEN ROOF INDUSTRY BACKGROUND

Green infrastructure was a vegetative system of green spaces and water systems designed to enhance the natural environment in urban settings. Green roofs, living walls, as well as parks and wetlands were all examples of green infrastructure. Green roof technology was initially refined in the 1970s by German horticulturists, architects, as well as structural and civil engineers, who had developed waterproofing technologies and blends of growing media that were lighter than soil. By the 1980s, Germany had passed a large number of local and federal laws encouraging green roof upgrades. Thirty years later, over a billion square feet of roof gardens had been installed in that country.[4]

Copyright © 2023 by the *Case Research Journal* and by Charla Mathwick. The author wishes to express appreciation to the reviewers and editors of the *Case Research Journal* for their thoughtful critique and helpful recommendations.

In contrast, commercial buildings in the United States were largely constructed during an era of extremely permissive building codes and low energy costs.[5] As a consequence, aging U.S. commercial and residential building stock was estimated to account for 36% of global energy use and nearly 40% of global greenhouse gas emissions.[6] The green roof movement began to migrate to the United States and Canada in the early 2000s as awareness of the effects of climate change grew. Engineers, architects, and landscape designers gradually adopted the techniques and building standards developed by their German counterparts.[7]

Green roofing systems were classified as either extensive or intensive gardens, with extensive green roofs being the most common, as well as the most utilitarian type. Extensive gardens utilized a shallow (3" to 6"; 7.5 to 15 cm) layer of growing media planted with low maintenance succulents. Known as sedum, these plants retained water and could withstand harsh rooftop growing conditions. Intensive roof gardens were planted with greater plant varieties including grasses, ground cover, flowers, shrubs, and trees which required 6" to 48" (15 to 120 cm) of growing media. Often designed to incorporate aesthetically elaborate landscaping features, intensive gardens included walking paths, benches, tables, and even basketball courts, transforming a rooftop into an urban green space, amenity deck, or a park designed for tenant use.[8]

Green roofing expanded the capacity of urban stormwater systems by serving as a sponge that slowed down rainwater runoff from building rooftops. Because roadways, drainage systems, and century-old stormwater sewers were made from impervious materials, an extreme downpour could send stormwater overflowing into the streets. For example, on September 2, 2021, the remnants of Hurricane Ida flooded the New York City subway system and basement apartments, causing $75 million in damage, and killing an estimated 43 people. Given the accelerating climate threat, city managers had begun to search for solutions to make their greying infrastructure more resilient.

TRENDS DRIVING DEMAND IN THE GREEN ROOF MARKET

CGT's expansion plans were shaped by the impact of emerging trends, particularly when the effect of those trends had the potential to influence stakeholder demand for green roofing materials. The B2B market that CGT operated in involved a drawn-out and complex buying process with diverse stakeholders exerting influence at various points in the sales cycle. Beyond the landscape architects and designers who worked directly with CGT, the decision to buy was also influenced by city, state, and federal government agencies, urban real estate developers, general contractors, civil engineers, as well as climate activists.

According to Green Roofs.org, a nonprofit association that worked to grow the green roofing industry, eleven North American cities had introduced mandates and nineteen city, state, and provincial governments had introduced incentive programs to encourage investment in green roof or living wall installations by 2019. Keitges and her team tracked the accelerating rollout of government mandates and incentive programs designed to bring trees and nature onto a building site. Increasingly, commercial builders had found they were unable to get through the permitting process without stormwater mitigation steps reflected in their plans.[9] Consequently, 75% of green roofs had been installed atop new commercial buildings (see **Exhibit 1a-b**).

When looking for new construction opportunities Keitges had learned to "follow the cranes," tracking commercial construction projects in major urban markets across North America.[10] For example, she considered the Rider Levett Bucknall (RLB) Crane Index which was based on a 14-city biannual count of the number of fixed cranes on construction sites. The RLB index provided a simplified metric to track urban construction activity. During Q1 2022, the RLB index was up 4.7% (e.g., 22 cranes) relative to the previous reporting period (**Exhibit 2**).

At the federal level, the Environmental Protection Agency (EPA) had become active in its effort to educate municipal governments as to the threat created by urban flooding from stormwater runoff emergencies.[11] Among other things, it distributed independent reports on infrastructure status. For example, in a 2021 study by the American Society of Civil Engineers, America's legacy stormwater infrastructure received an overall grade of "D," in part due to the $9 billion in damage that resulted from urban flooding annually (see **Exhibit 3**).[12]

The eighty-five percent of the U.S. population that lived in metropolitan areas had also become increasingly vulnerable to 'heat island' effects. The concentration of buildings, paved roads, and parking lots retained heat and caused high-density cities to be 15° to 20° hotter than nearby areas with more trees and less pavement. According to the EPA, urban heat islands increased energy consumption, elevated emissions from air pollutants and greenhouse gases, compromised human health, and degraded water quality.

Keitges was well-aware of the positive effect a green roof could have on urban environments, explaining, "you can literally fry an egg on rooftop surfaces. We found that urban rooftop temperatures can range anywhere from 120° to 140° during summer months. But when you install a green roof, temperatures drop to 80°."

Climate Central, a nonprofit research organization composed of climate scientists, television meteorologists, and journalists, published an annual index reflecting the intensity of urban heat islands. Their 2021 analysis indicated the five most intense urban heat islands in the U.S. were in New Orleans, Newark, New York City, Houston, and San Francisco (**Exhibit 4**).[13]

CGT BACKGROUND

Although the green roofing industry in the U.S. was fragmented, CGT had grown to dominate the West Coast market by 2022. One of CGT's early 'wins' included a partnership with Firestone, which produced a roofing membrane used in commercial building applications. CGT execs also landed a green roofing deal with retail giant Walmart and had begun to export into the Canadian market. Keitges described the early days of CGT's entry into the green roof market this way:

> Only 1% of the small businesses in America export. But because CGT had sold into Vancouver B.C. and Toronto, where a lot of green roofing was being installed, we won the 2013-14 U.S. Department of Commerce Export Award. As a result, during the fall of 2013, I was appointed to President Obama's Export Council,[14] where I represented the interests of small business and the green building industry. Keitges joined twenty-six other CEOs from large corporations including Boeing, Disney, IBM, Merck, and e-Bay, to report to the President of the United States biannually.

> From there, Keitges went on to be nominated as one of the "Top 40 under 40" executives in Oregon and was mentioned as a top woman in "technology to invest in" by Forbes.[15]

We were very fortunate," conceded Keitges, "as a woman working in the green construction industry, all that recognition gave us access to early-stage capital and a platform to grow on. Being in the right place, at the right time, with the smartest team in the industry, helped us raise our initial rounds of funding."

CGT's Product Features & Service Partnerships

Keitges boasted about having spent "zero on marketing," relying instead on a referral-based business model with references that came from satisfied customers sourced by the CGT sales team. The company had developed a downloadable brochure detailing its modular product design, which could be customized to project specifications (see **Exhibit 5**). CGT's two product lines utilized a patented interlocking system of planting trays with built-in irrigation, micro-holes to manage stormwater, and ridges to allow air flow. Its proprietary growing media was 40% to 50% of the weight of traditional garden soil, but stable enough to support plant growth in the high wind and harsh weather conditions found on urban rooftops.

Cost savings were a significant source of value delivered by CGT's solutions. "We became a recognized player in the industry once we demonstrated we could save building owners money by managing stormwater on their rooftops rather than holding runoff in concrete underground storage tanks," explained Keitges. CGT also offered the ease of a full-service solution by leveraging partnerships with various firms along its value chain. For example, nurseries on the West and East Coast partnered with CGT, utilizing its growing media to pre-plant trays filled with local plant varieties customized to landscape designer and architect specifications. Nursery partners also offered CGT's pre-planted sedum tiles, a product that was installed like sod.

CGT managed the logistics process behind a green roof installation, ensuring the roofing materials, as well as the commercial cranes needed to lift those materials onto rooftop construction sites, aligned with builder schedules. Installation was outsourced to local crews certified by CGT. Although the entire process involved local partners, clients perceived a full-service, one-stop customer experience. Consequently, building a localized presence had become a key driver behind the expansion strategy.

With over a decade in business, CGT had demonstrated the cost effectiveness, ease of installation, and reliability of its system. "When you're talking about construction materials, reliable performance is essential. One of the biggest hurdles in the green roof material-sales process was overcoming concerns about roof leaks," explained Keitges. To reinforce confidence in its system, CGT offered a 20-year warranty that covered the full green roof assembly, backed by a warranty to cover the cost of removal and restoration in the event of a leak.

The Retro-Fit Market

Urban water departments typically grandfathered the stormwater sewer system connections of existing buildings. However, should those building owners decide to remodel, the permitting process required them to upgrade their stormwater infrastructure. Consequently, commercial retrofit construction presented an opportunity to grow beyond the 25% of the market it currently comprised. Underutilized rooftops represented millions of acres of future green roof development in the retrofit portion of the market alone.[16]

Demand for green roof installation on existing buildings received a boost in 2021 as building owners grappled with the challenge of getting people back into the office following the COVID-19 lockdowns.[17] Employers discovered they could lure employees back to the office by bringing natural environments into the workplace with green roofs that created opportunities for outdoor lunch breaks, special events, or walking meetings in a park-like setting. Columbia Green's COO/CFO, Deni Blumhardt was excited about the retrofit opportunity. "We are seeing amenity decks built for reasons other than simply managing runoff. A green roof installation appeals to building tenants because it provides a view onto beautiful rooftop environments while delivering higher margins for us. It is a win on a lot of levels."

One of the highest-profile examples of a Columbia Green retrofit installation was the 'Meadow,' a 125-year-old building in the heart of Chicago. According to Kyle DeLuna, VP at Jones Lang LaSalle, a real estate and investment services firm headquartered in Chicago, "Columbia Green was critical to the success of the country's largest private roof deck, which was installed on top of the Old Post Office building." Describing CGT's contribution to the project, DeLuna explained,

> Vanessa Keitges and the entire Columbia Green team brought a much-welcomed value-add to our project for a variety of reasons. From the bidding process, through the execution of the work, the service was phenomenal . . . . CGT partnered with certified landscape installers, [providing] the expertise required for a project that involved over 3,000 helicopter lifts for delivery of the structural and landscaping components. The project transformed the rooftop of the Old Post Office building into a 3.5-acre park, 10 stories up in downtown Chicago … a major success.

The Meadow not only absorbed, retained, and filtered more than a quarter-million gallons of stormwater annually, it also served as a massive insulating blanket, reducing building energy costs. The urban pollinator population was also reinvigorated as beehives placed on the site produced more than one hundred gallons of honey, shared with local food pantries annually.[18]

The STAKEHOLDER'S ROLE IN CGT'S SALES CYCLE

The process of initially drawing up a commercial construction plan through project completion typically spanned multiple years. Green roof installations were the final phase of that process. Consequently, CGT's strategic sales and business development directors collaborated with architects and civil engineers to drive specifications in the early days of a new project, sometimes years before the sales team got involved. Being written into the original specifications meant a company like CGT would be identified as a preferred vendor. "That, more than anything else, made our life easier and our sales cycle shorter," explained Blumhardt

CGT had two sales reps on the West Coast and one in the Washington DC area to cover the Mid-Atlantic region. Andrea Saven, its Technical Director, was a landscape architect located at headquarters in Portland. She was involved with product development and educational outreach at industry conferences, tradeshows, and through continuing education designed to satisfy licensing requirements in the landscape design community. "I think of landscape designers, architects, and civil engineers as our customers," explained Saven. "Although designers don't necessarily write the checks, they are the ones who respond to a builder's request for proposal (RFP) and the architects and civil engineers identify us in their initial building specs."

Landscape architecture and design was a $7 billion industry with 1.5% annual growth forecasted through 2027, which made the green roofing market an attractive business opportunity. As of 2022, an estimated 42,642 landscape design firms operated in the U.S., however, a quarter of industry revenues went to the five top firms (see

Exhibit 6).[19] Consequently, the office locations of the biggest landscape design or architectural firms were a factor in the salesforce expansion plan.

In B2B markets, stakeholders played a crucial role, shaping brand awareness by sharing their impressions online or through referrals.[20] The challenge was to get CGT's message out to the architects, landscape designers, engineers, and developers in its market. In a single client meeting, a civil engineer or city environmental services manager might raise questions about stormwater management. The landscape architects might ask about integrating native plants into the sedum pallets to earn additional LEED credits[a] or have questions related to solar panel integration. CGT also collaborated with architects and engineers to ensure green roof assemblies met structural load requirements.

> The hardest piece for us, and why I am seeking investment to scale, is the need for education about these different facets of our business. The unique expertise our team brings to this process is a genuine competitive advantage. Nonetheless, if you want to make an impact in a market where a convergence of trends is creating double digit growth, you need to go after capital, scale your business, and do it fast, explained Keitges.

As Blumhardt put it, "we were planning to build out our sales teams in locations where demand was heating up." The plan was to increase the sales force fourfold over the next year to capture demand in high-growth markets. The first step in building out the funding pitch, however, was to identify and prioritize geographic markets according to potential. Everyone understood that defending the growth assumptions would be key.

Time to get the details down in writing!

---

[a] LEED® certification (Leadership in Energy & Environmental Design) requires a building project earn a minimum number of credits by adopting sustainable strategies aligned with energy efficient, water saving materials, indoor environmental quality, design innovation, and regional priorities. Green roofs qualify for 6 – 14 LEED credits.

Exhibit 1a: Green Roof Mandatory Policies and/or Incentive Program Implementation [b]

Cities and/or States	Mandatory Green Roof Policies	Green Roof Incentive Programs
Adams County, CO		2014
Austin, TX		2014
Baltimore, MD		2012
Chicago, Illinois	2014 and 2017	2015
Denver, CO	2017	
Boston, MA	2012, 2013, 2014	
Fife, WA	2009	
Fort Wayne, IN		2018
Guelph, ON		2018
Hoboken, NJ		2018
Indianapolis, IN		2016
Milwaukee, WI		2018
Minneapolis, MN		2017
Montgomery County, MD		2018
Nashville, TN		2016
New York City	2019	2013 and 2017
Palo Alto, CA		2017
Philadelphia, PA		2015
Portland, ME		2015
Portland, OR	2018	
Baltimore, MD		2013
St. Laurent, Quebec	2016	
San Francisco, CA	2017 and 2019	
Seattle, WA	2007	2009
Syracuse, NY		2018
Toronto, Ontario	2009	2016
Washington, DC	2012 and 2017	2013, 2016 and 2018

[b] Exhibits 1a-b compiled by Author from: Maya Stern, Steven W. Peck, and Jeff Joslin (2019). "Green Roof and Wall Policy in North America: Regulations, Incentives, and Best Practices (2019)." Green Roofs for Healthy Cities, p. 14-15. Accessed July 11, 2022 from https://static1.squarespace.com/static/58e3eecf2994ca997dd56381/t/5d84dfc371cf0822bdf7d c29/1568989140101/Green_Roof_and_Wall_Policy_in_North_America.pdf

Exhibit 1b: Municipal Stormwater Regulatory Phase (MS4)[21]

Cities and or States	Date Instituted	Assessing Barriers to (GI) Green Infrastructure (1)	Stormwater Standards Establish-- Focus on GI Education (2)	GI Regulatory Mandates Implemented (3)
MA	7/2018			✓
NH	7/2018			✓
Burlington, VT	7/2018			✓
Baltimore, MD	12/2013			✓
DC	6/2018			✓
Atlanta, GA	6//2019			✓
Louisville, KY	2/2017		✓	
Chattanooga, TN	1/2011		✓	
Nashville, TN	2/2012			✓
Chicago, IL	3/2016			✓
New Mexico	12//2014			✓
Oklahoma	6/2021	✓		
Denver, CO	7/2016		✓	
Montana	1/2017	✓		
Utah	5/2021			✓
CA: LA	12/2012			✓
CA	7/2013		✓	
CA: SF Bay	1/2016		✓	
Honolulu, HI	9/2020		✓	
OR	3/2019		✓	
Seattle, WA	8/2019		✓	
WA	8/2019		✓	

Exhibit 2: RLB Crane Index (Q1, 2022)[c]

City	Development Type
Boston (Reduction in Cranes)	Life Sciences, Multi-Family, Mixed Use Projects
Calgary, Canada (Steady Crane Count)	Residential projects drive demand
Chicago (3 Crane Increase)	High-rise Luxury Rental Condos
Denver (Increase in Cranes)	Apartments Mixed Use
Honolulu (1 Crane Increase)	Luxury High Rise Condos/Mixed Use
Las Vegas (Steady Crane Count)	Hospitality and Municipal Building
Los Angeles (Steady Crane Count)	Multi-Family & Mixed Use Projects (67%)
New York City (Slight Increase)	Commercial/Financial
Phoenix (Steady Crane Count)	Residential Apartments Multi-Family/Mixed Use
Portland (Decrease in Cranes)	Mixed Use/Residential Sr./Affordable Housing
San Francisco (Increased Cranes)	Residential and Mixed-Use Development Industrial & Commercial
Seattle (Steady Crane Count)	Residential sites Education Healthcare Facilities Commercial
Toronto, Ontario (Increased Cranes)	Commercial/Residential/Mixed
Washington, DC (Decline in Cranes)	Hospitality Residential Mixed Use Projects

---

[c] Compiled by the Author from Cathy Sewell (March 29, 2022). "RLB Crane Index., North America" Accessed July 19, 2022 from https://www.rlb.com/americas/insight/rlb-crane-index-north-america-q1-2022/

Exhibit 3: American Society of Civil Engineer's 2021 Stormwater Report Card[d]

STATE (City)	Stormwater Fee/month to fund stormwater system upgrades. National Avg Stormwater Fee=$5.87*	Stormwater Infrastructure Grade *
AZ, Phoenix	Stormwater Fee: ($3.09) Local flood districts typically performed the necessary operation and maintenance of these stormwater structures to ensure public safety of communities. The average age of a levee in Arizona was 41 years old. It is likely that only a small percentage of levee owners in the state had adequate funding to address the estimated $10 to $20 million needed per year for repairs, upkeep, and upgrades.	C to C-
CA, Los Angeles	Stormwater Fee: ($4.12) Stormwater infrastructure in California included legacy systems as well as green infrastructure. The drainage infrastructure was largely constructed prior to the 1940s, putting it near the end of its useful life. Further, the new and innovative drainage systems, necessary to meet water quality standards and promote a sustainable environment, were significantly underfunded. For example, over the next 20 years in Los Angeles County, the cost of achieving water quality objectives was estimated at about $20 billion, and in San Diego County, it was estimated at about $5 billion.	D+
CO, Denver	Stormwater Fee: ($8.01) No Specific Stormwater Report	C-
DC, Washington	Stormwater Fee: ($2.67) No Specific Stormwater Report	C
FL, Miami	Stormwater Fee: ($6.64) 35% of municipalities reported having a stormwater program to fund and maintain the infrastructure, with a $14 million funding shortfall per stormwater entity by 2023. In May 2021 legislation designated $500 million to support the implementation of projects in the Statewide Flooding and Sea Level Rise Resilience Plan.	C-
HI, Honolulu	Stormwater Fee: ($0.00) In recent years, Hawaii had experienced an increase in extreme flooding caused by high tides, storm surges, hurricane rainfall, tsunamis, and sea level rise. Hawaii's stormwater systems drained directly into the ocean, affecting marine life. Based on the Environmental Protection Agency's 2018 assessment, 88 of the 108 marine water bodies did not meet water quality standards.	D-

---

[d] American Society of Civil Engineers (2021). State Infrastructure Rankings. Accessed Sept 30, 2022 from State Infrastructure Rankings | ASCE's 2021 Infrastructure Report Card

IL, Chicago	Stormwater Fee: ($5.00) Stormwater infrastructure was aging and undersized given increased rainfall trends. With population growth, and urban flooding due to rainfall trends, Illinois' current stormwater systems would not have sufficient capacity to meet future needs. Additional funding and resources would be needed to repair, upgrade, and/or replace these systems.	**D+**
IN, Fort Wayne	Stormwater Fee: ($6.25) No Specific Stormwater Report	**C- (overall)**
MA, Boston	Stormwater Fee: ($5.80) No Specific Stormwater Report	**C- (overall)**
MD, Baltimore	Stormwater Fee: ($5.87) The Maryland stormwater management efforts were regarded as some of the most innovative nationwide, with upgrades underway since 2000. However, the Chesapeake Bay water quality had been steadily declining over the last few decades. In 2010, new limits on the level of pollutants that could enter the body of water were set, but statewide stormwater costs to comply with these regulations were projected to be more than $3 billion. The cost of building supporting infrastructure mostly fell to local municipalities and the state, with limited resources.	**C (overall)**
ME, Portland	Stormwater Fee: ($5.51) Within the past five decades, extreme precipitation events increased by 70% which was more significant than in any other U.S. region. Urban stormwater disproportionately impacted Maine's surface water quality, considering that only 2.8% of the state was developed land.	**C-**
MN, Minneapolis	Stormwater Fee: ($7.37) No separate stormwater report.	**C (overall)**
NV, Las Vegas	Stormwater Fee: ($7.77) Nevada experienced severe flash flooding from rapid snow melt or short duration, high-intensity thunderstorms, creating significant stormwater runoff problems. The state invested in a $868 million, 10-year construction program which was primarily funded by quarter-cent sales tax and bonds. In Northern Nevada, the $400 million Truckee River Flood Project included levees, floodwalls, terracing, bridge replacement, and mitigation measures. However, statewide, there continued to be projected funding shortfalls upwards of $400 million for necessary flood mitigation projects.	**C**
NY, New York	Stormwater Fee: ($4.75) No Specific Stormwater Report Wastewater - Aging sewer infrastructure led to increased infiltration and inflow, broken pipes, clogging, exfiltration, and equipment failures. These occurrences stressed a system that was already at or near its capacity, causing sewer overflows.	**C (overall)** **D+ wastewater**

OR, Portland	Stormwater Fee: ($7.22) No Specific Stormwater Report Demand had substantially increased on aging infrastructure on the brink of failure, a concern magnified by the earthquake threat. Many of the wastewater systems were beyond useful design life and would soon need replacement or full rehabilitation. Estimates showed a $5 billion investment needed for Oregon's wastewater infrastructure alone.	
PA, Philadelphia	Stormwater Fee: ($7.17) Pennsylvania's stormwater infrastructure was 100+ years old, and needed on-going repairs, replacement, and capacity upgrades. In 2013 PA created a stormwater authority, and in 2016 empowered local governments to apply a stormwater use-based revenue system to fund the operation, maintenance, and upgrades to stormwater assets. PA was the state with the most combined sewer overflows, with billions of gallons of untreated sewage entering streams annually.	**D to D-**
TN, Nashville	Stormwater Fee: ($3.58) No specific stormwater report	
TX, Austin	Stormwater Fee: ($4.77) No specific stormwater report 10% of Texas population was exposed to moderate or high annual flood risks. In 2019, the state initiated a State Flood Plan with $1.8 billion funding for new, statewide flood risk mitigation which includes stormwater management. The magnitude of Texas' need was significant, exceeding $31.5 billion over the next decade.	**C to C-** **(overall)**
WA, Seattle	Stormwater Fees: ($12.18) Stormwater fees were collected to manage the cost of King County's treatment plant for polluted stormwater; Tacoma's treatment facility to protect residential neighborhoods, and Puget Sound. Seattle started construction on a $570 million combined sewer overflow storage project to reduce untreated stormwater and wastewater flows to the Lake Washington Shipping Canal. Much of the stormwater infrastructure was beyond its design life.	**D+**
WI, Milwaukee	Stormwater Fees: ($5.47) 120 Wisconsin municipalities implemented stormwater fee collection to bolster funding levels to deal with municipal stormwater	**C**

* A stormwater fee is a charge imposed on real estate owners for pollution resulting from rainwater runoff and to cover the costs of maintaining stormwater drainage systems. The fee varies by locale but is generally based on total impervious area, which includes concrete, asphalt driveways, and rooftops on the property, measured as equivalent residential units (ERU). The more area covered by impervious surfaces, the more stormwater runoff generated and the higher the fee. Stormwater fees are based on a charge per ERU.[22]**When a stormwater-specific grade was not available, the overall infrastructure grade for that city/state was used.

Exhibit 4: Climate Central's Heat Island Index: Top 20 U.S. Cities[e]

City	Index Score (Fahrenheit)*
1. New Orleans	8.94
2. Newark, NJ	7.71
3. New York City	7.62
4. Houston	7.46
5. San Francisco	7.37
6. Boston	7.24
7. Chicago	7.24
8. Miami	7.24
9. Baltimore, MD	7.08
10. Providence, RI	7.08
11. Sacramento, CA	7.08
12. Salinas, CA	7.08
13. Burlington, VT	7.08
14. Bend, OR	6.97
15. Cleveland, OH	6.97
16. Detroit, MI	6.97
17. Erie, PA	6.97
18. Fresno, CA	6.97
19. Lafayette, LA	6.97
20. McAllen, TX	6.97

*The index score for a city is a temperature increase above average, showing the potential difference in average temperature for the city compared to its surroundings. Urban temperatures measured ranged from less than 5°F to nearly 9°F. Each score is an average for the entire city, consequently, certain neighborhoods or areas of a city will likely be cooler or hotter, depending on vegetation and other factors.

[e] Research Brief by Climate Central (July 14, 2021). Hot Zones: Urban Heat Islands," Climate Central. Accessed July 19, 2022 from https://www.climatecentral.org/climate-matters/urban-heat-islands. Full Report: 2021_UHI_Report.pdf (ctfassets.net), p. 3-4.

Exhibit 5 - Columbia Green Technologies 2022 Brochure

Source: https://columbia-green.com/wp-content/uploads/2022/01/Columbia-Green_Brochure.pdf

Columbia Green Technologies offers the most innovative vegetated roof systems on the market. In addition to our green roof products, we are a complete amenity deck provider- offering pavers, pedestals, and foam. Our green roofs create beautiful, soothing views, improve our environment, and help drive the 'green' and ESG economy.

BENEFITS OF A GREEN ROOF

Columbia Green's green roof systems decrease carbon emissions and building energy use, reduce the heat island effect and provide stormwater management. Green roofs soak up rain, decreasing runoff to prevent flooding in cities worldwide. Columbia Green is committed to creating a positive environmental and social impact, helping build vibrant healthy cities.

- Reduce and delay stormwater runoff, helping cities struggling with aging storm and sewer infrastructure. Green Roofs naturally soak up the rain and prevent flooding.

- Add plant biodiversity and provide habitat for pollinator species.

- Protects the roof membrane and at least doubles the life of the roof.

- Bring year-round building energy savings - as a thermal blanket- providing cost savings on building's heating and cooling.

- Green roofs reduce the air temperature through evapotranspiration, reducing the urban heat island effect.

- Health & Wellness: Green roofs can help reduce stress, anxiety, depression by providing access to air, light, and nature.

THE COLUMBIA GREEN COMPLETE PACKAGE:

PAVERS • PEDESTALS • STYROFOAM™ • GEOFOAM • ROOT BARRIER • METAL EDGERS • SLOPED

LAYERED SYSTEM
Our Built-in-Place System for Extensive and Intensive

» Columbia Green Growing Media, regionally blended

» Soil depth flexibility: from 3-inch media depth (extensive) to 48-inches+ media depth (amenity decks).

» Water Retention Layer, provides supplemental moisture retention for plants. Available in .5-inch or 1-inch thickness

» Drainage Layer to prevent ponding and move excess water efficiently to the nearest drain. Available in .375-inch and .75-inch thickness

» Metal Edger for perimeter stability.

» Layered system sits on Columbia Green Rootbarrier

TRAY SYSTEMS
Pre-Grown and Planted-in-Place (with optional drip irrigation)

» Patented interlocking and overlapping tray design

» Tray designed by landscape architects, stormwater engineers, horticulturists and roofing experts

» Simple installation

» Plants can be planted on-site or pregrown

» Tray is designed to maximize stormwater retention

» *Integrated drip irrigation* available

» Tray sits on Columbia Green Slip-Sheet

» Soil depth range 4-5/8 inches to 8-inches

COLUMBIA GREEN EDGER
PLANT MATERIAL
COLUMBIA GREEN GROWING MEDIA
COLUMBIA GREEN WATER RETENTION LAYER
COLUMBIA GREEN DRAINAGE/FILTRATION LAYER
COLUMBIA GREEN ROOT BARRIER
ROOF ASSEMBLY, BY OTHERS

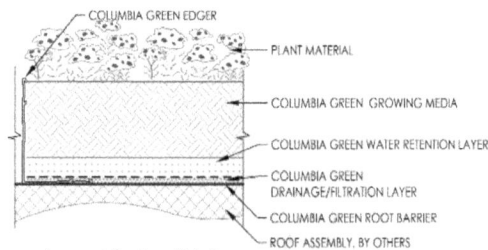

Layered System Detail

FLEXIBLE DEPTH COLUMBIA GREEN GROWING MEDIA DEPTH

PLANTING OPTIONS: COLUMBIA GREEN PREGROWN SEDUM, CUTTINGS, PLUGS OR ACCENT PERENNIALS

PATENTED INTERLOCKING TRAYS, PREVENT SHIFTING, GROWING MEDIA SPILLAGE AND PROTECT AGAINST WIND UPLIFT.

TRAY STRUCTURE ALLOWS FOR DRAINAGE AND AIR FLOW. MICRO-DRAIN HOLES INCREASE WATER RETENTION

COLUMBIA GREEN SLIP SHEET

ROOF ASSEMBLY BY OTHERS

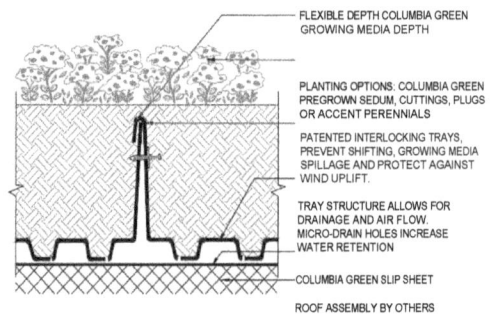

Planted in Place System Detail

Pregrown Sedum   Perennials & Shrubs   Plugs   Sedum Cuttings

PLAZA DECK PAVERS

Ask us about our array of Paver and Pedestal options to fit every project.

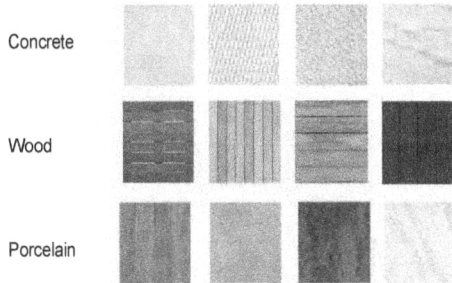

Concrete

Wood

Porcelain

OUR TECHNICAL EXPERTISE & DESIGN SUPPORT

- Stormwater Retention Calculations
- Standard and Custom Details
- Specifications
- Regional Plants & Growing Media Expertise
- System Weight Calculations
- Wind Uplift
- Green roofs with Solar
- Budgetary Information
- Maintenance Guidelines

Contact Us:
Columbia Green National Headquarters
503.327.8723 | info@columbia-green.com
Offices in the Northeast, Mid-Atlantic, West and Midwest

WARRANTIES

Standard Full System Warranty

Our systems come with a standard Full System Warranty with an optional Overburden Warranty.

Overburden Removal Warranty

Covering the cost of removing and replacing the green roof system, pavers, insulation, foam, and pedestals in the event of a roof leak.

FOAM AND INSULATION

Many options for lightweight rooftop structural fill and insulation: XPS Insulation, EPS Geofoam and NEW Recycled Foam Glass Aggregate- a lightweight, load-bearing 'gravel' used under landscape mounds, pavers and in planters.

COLUMBIA GREEN
TECHNOLOGIES

Exhibit 6[f]: Top Landscape/Architectural Design Firms in U.S.

Landscape Design Firms	West Coast	Gulf Coast & Southeast	Mid-Atlantic	Midwest, Mt. & Southwest
Brightview Holdings	48 locations	18 locations in Texas; 7 in GA, 5 in SC; 29 in FL	7 locations in NY, 8 in MD; 10 in DC/VA;	5 locations in IL; 7 in CO
Gensler	Los Angeles, Newport Beach, Oakland, Portland, Seattle, San Diego, San Francisco, San Jose, Vancouver	Atlanta, , Charlotte, Austin, Dallas, Houston, San Antonio, Miami, Tampa,	Baltimore, Boston, Philadelphia, Morristown, NJ, Nashville, NY, Toronto, Washington, DC	Chicago, Denver, Detroit, Lacrosse, Las Vegas, Minneapolis, Phoenix
HDR, Inc.	West Coast: CA 17 locations; 8 in WA, 4 in OR	11 locations in FL, 11 in TX	4 locations in Washington DC, 4 in NY, 5 in PA	
Perkins and Will, Inc.	Bainbridge Island, WA			
Hammel, Green & Abrahamson	4 locations in CA		Washington, DC, VA, MA	2 locations in MN, 2 in WI
HKS, Inc.	Los Angeles, San Diego, San Francisco	Atlanta, Austin, Dallas, Ft. Worth, Houston, Orlando, Miami, Raleigh, NC	New York, Richmond, VA, Washington, DC	Chicago, Detroit, Phoenix, Salt Lake
Hok Group, Inc.	Los Angeles, San Francisco, Seattle	New York, Philadelphia, DC	Atlanta, Dallas, Houston, Miami, Tampa	Chicago, Columbus, Denver, Kansas City, St. Louis
Sasaki Assoc.			Boston, New York	Denver
Kohn Pederson Fox Associates	San Francisco		New York	
NBBJ	Los Angeles, Portland, San Francisco, Seattle		Boston, New York, DC	
Forrest Perkins, Inc.	Los Angeles	Dallas	New York, Washington, DC	

[f] Complied by Author from Cesar Maldonado (June 2022). "Landscape Design in the U.S." IBIS World.com, Accessed Sept 27, 2022 from https://my-ibisworld-com.proxy.lib.pdx.edu/us/en/industry/54132/about

REFERENCES

[1] Contrive Datum Insights (2022). "Green Roof Market Size, Share, & Trends Estimation Report (Extensive, Intensive) by Application (Residential, Commercial, Industrial), by Region and Segment Forecasts, 2023 – 2030. Accessed March 16, 2023 from https://www.contrivedatuminsights.com/product-report/green-roof-market-248402/?Mode=TM OR https://www.globenewswire.com/news-release/2023/01/27/2596592/0/en/Green-Roof-Market-is-Expected-to-Grow-at-a-CAGR-of-16-20-Reaching-a-Valuation-of-US-5-37-Billion-from-2022-2030-Contrive-Datum-Insights.html

[2] Deladerriere, Alexis (March 28, 2022). "What Sustainability Themes Are You Currently Excited About?" Goldman Sachs Asset Management. Accessed June 9, 2022 from https://www.gsam.com/content/gsam/are/en/advisors/market-insights/gsam-connect/2021/environmental-sustainability-an-inflection-point-for-investors.html).

[3] Davis, Dominic-Madori (January 18, 2023). "Women-founded startups raised 1.9% of all VC funds in 2022, a drop from 2021," TechCrunch +. Accessed March 16, 2023 from https://techcrunch.com/2023/01/18/women-founded-startups-raised-1-9-of-all-vc-funds-in-2022-a-drop-from-2021/

[4] Wolff, Fiona (Fall, 2021). "Insights into Germany's Green Roof and Wall Market," Trends, and Policy," Living Architecture Academy. Accessed Sept 25, 2022 from Insight Into Germany's Green Roof and Wall Market, Trends, and Policy (livingarchitecturemonitor.com)

[5] Feldstein, Stuart A. (2021). "Age of U.S. Commercial Buildings," SMR Research Corporation. Accessed July 13, 2022 from https://www.commbuildings.com/ResearchComm.html

[6] International Energy Agency (IEA; 2020). "Energy Efficiency 2020: Buildings," IEA.org, Paris. Accessed July 12, 2022 from https://www.iea.org/reports/energy-efficiency-2020/buildings

[7] DiNardo, Kelly (Oct 9, 2019). "The Green Revolution Spreading Across our Rooftops," TheNewYorkTimes.com. Accessed July 28 2022 from https://www.nytimes.com/2019/10/09/realestate/the-green-roof-revolution.html

[8] "Columbia Green's AVRS Tray Installation," Columbia Green Technologies. Accessed Sept 15, 2022 from (https://www.youtube.com/watch?v=nz_6tnnK0uM&ab_channel=ColumbiaGreen AVRS).

[9] Office of Wastewater Management, Water Permits Division (June, 2022). "Compendium of MS4 Permitting Approaches," EPA.gov. EPA-833-B-22-002. Accessed October 28, 2022 from https://www.epa.gov/system/files/documents/2022-06/Green%20Infrastructure%20MS4%20Compendium%202022_1.pdf

[10] Sewell, Cathy (March 29, 2022). "RLB Crane Index., North America" Accessed July 19, 2022 from https://www.rlb.com/americas/insight/rlb-crane-index-north-america-q1-2022/

[11] U.S. Environmental Protection Agency (Aug. 9, 2022). "Why you should consider green stormwater infrastructure for your community," EPA.gov. Accessed Sept. 9,

2022 from https://www.epa.gov/G3/why-you-should-consider-green-stormwater-infrastructure-your-community

12 Infrastructure Report Card.org. "2021 Infrastructure Report Card," Accessed on Sept. 9, 2022 from https://infrastructurereportcard.org/cat-item/stormwater-infrastructure/

13 Research Brief by Climate Central (July 14, 2021). Hot Zones: Urban Heat Islands," Climate Central. Accessed July 19, 2022 from https://www.climatecentral.org/climate-matters/urban-heat-islands

14 Business Wire (Sept 20, 2013). "Vanessa Keitges, CEO Columbia Green Technologies, Named to President's Export Council." Accessed March 15, 2023 from https://www.businesswire.com/news/home/20130920005167/en/Vanessa-Keitges-CEO-Columbia-Green-Technologies-Named-to-President%E2%80%99s-Export-Council

15 Brodock, Kate (May 3, 2012). "5 Women-led Tech Companies to Invest In," Forbes.com. Accessed March, 2023 from 5 Women-led Tech Companies To Invest In (forbes.com)

16 Stern, Maya, Steve W. Peck, and Jeff Joslin (2019). "Green Roof and Wall Policy in North America: Regulations, Incentives, and Best Practices," Green Roofs for Healthy Cities. Accessed July 11, 2022 from https://static1.squarespace.com/static/58e3eecf2994ca997dd56381/t/5d84dfc371cf0822bdf7dc29/1568989140101/Green_Roof_and_Wall_Policy_in_North_America.pdf

17 Wolfrom, Jessica (Dec, 22, 2021 updated May 26, 2022). "The ecological promise of living roofs and walls". SF Eaminer.com. Accessed June 10, 2022 from https://www.sfexaminer.com/the_fs/fixes/the-ecological-promise-of-living-roofs-and-walls/article_0e7e359b-8f77-5761-a5be-9b40ab06aeff.html

18 Holmes, Damian (April 6, 2022). The Meadow at Old Chicago Post Office," worldlandscapearchitect.com. Accessed July 14, 2022 from https://worldlandscapearchitect.com/green-roofs-for-healthy-cities-old-chicago-post-office/

19 Maldonado, Cesar (June 2022). "Landscape Design in the U.S." Ibis World.com, Accessed Sept 27, 2022 from https://my-ibisworld-com.proxy.lib.pdx.edu/us/en/industry/54132/about

20 Iglesias et al. (2020). "Corporate brand identity co-creation in business-to-business contexts," Industrial Marketing Management, 85, 32-43.

21 Office of Wastewater Management, Water Permits Division (June, 2022). "Compendium of MS4 Permitting Approaches," EPA.gov. EPA-833-B-22-002, p 7-9. Accessed October 28, 2022 from https://www.epa.gov/system/files/documents/2022-06/Green%20Infrastructure%20MS4%20Compendium%202022_1.pdf

22 American Society of Civil Engineers (2021). State Infrastructure Rankings. Accessed Sept 30, 2022 from State Infrastructure Rankings | ASCE's 2021 Infrastructure Report Card

Dr. Wehrheim Winery: To Grow or Not to Grow?

Marc Dressler, Ludwigshafen University of Applied Sciences
Ram Subramanian, Stetson University

Late in the afternoon on a day in June 2022, Franz Wehrheim, fourth-generation member of the Dr. Wehrheim Winery (Wehrheim) winemaker located in the Palatinate region of Germany, realized that he had a decision to make. At the end of a spirited debate on the pros and cons of growing the winery at lunch earlier that day, his father, Karl-Heinz[1], had asked him to develop a recommendation with a strong rationale for Franz's idea of growing the business by sourcing grapes via a long-term partnership. This would create a second set of offerings to complement the winery's premium line of wines that were produced with grapes grown in the family's vineyards. While Karl-Heinz was quite skeptical of growth in this manner, because of its impact on quality, he was willing to change his mind if Franz presented a compelling narrative.

With revenues of a little over €1 million in 2020, Wehrheim competed in the German wine market where more than half the annual sales came from foreign competitors. Franz saw an opportunity to grow the business by taking market share away from imported wines. To Franz, volume expansion offered the opportunity to win new customers, increase prices, and reduce risks by channel diversification. His father resisted what he considered excessive growth ambitions, as he feared a potential loss of reputation and likely delivery risks for the small winery during lower yield years. What triggered the lunch discussion was an approach by Franz's college friend who expressed an interest in selling grapes to Wehrheim. Franz, who had already researched growth via market expansion by this time, saw this overture as an attractive opportunity for the wine estate to grow and eventually create a secondary wine. Indeed, Franz felt that this could help establish new contracts with nationwide retail chains that would help draw interest in Wehrheim´s flagship wines. Since the family winery made important business decisions at an annual strategy retreat, Karl-Heinz had made it clear to Franz that, while he was against volume growth, he was willing to keep an open mind and be persuaded if Franz presented his recommendations at the annual strategy retreat that was to be held in four weeks' time. The decision on whether to proceed with the secondary line would be made at the upcoming retreat.

As Franz reflected on the upcoming decision, he thought about his role and contribution to the family winery:

> At this point in time, my father is transitioning the ownership of the winery to me. He is still the controlling owner, but I hope to take over control in the near future. While I am responsible for sales and marketing, I want to move on to deciding on the winery's strategy. I have talked to my father about this,

---

and he is willing, though a bit cautious. I realize that the decision to grow Wehrheim fairly aggressively is something that I came up with and to get my father's support for it, I have to offer him a sound rationale. I see the strategic future of the winery as important, both for the family and for my leadership of the business.

THE GERMAN WINE MARKET

Germany ranked 4th in global wine consumption with an annual consumption of about two billion liters (see **Exhibit 1** for country-wise wine consumption). Neighboring wine-producing countries, especially France and Spain, suffered an ongoing decline in wine consumption. German wineries had historically reached directly to wine consumers but, starting in the late 1990s, retail was increasing its market share (see **Exhibit 2** for wine sales in Germany by channel). Starting in 2020, online sales of specialized wine retailers and wineries´ e-business increased, fueled by the Covid-19 pandemic. German wineries faced competition not only internally but also from international wine producers. International wines comprised more than half of German wine consumption. Imported wines competed across the price spectrum, with wines from Italy, Spain, and France the top sellers. While German wine consumers were highly price-sensitive (**Exhibit 3** lists the average price of a mid-range bottle of wine by country), a magazine observed that the
presence of wine enthusiasts with mature and diverse tastes, and openness to imports, made the country a challenging market for domestic producers.[2]

The Palatinate region constituted the second-largest German wine area (**Exhibit 4** shows Germany's wine-producing regions). Together with the largest wine region (Rhineland), the two regions made up 50% of German production area. Riesling and Pinot Noir[3] were the most popular grape varietals. On a grapevine area of 103,000 hectares, Germany produced between 8 and 11 million hectoliters (1 hectoliter equaled 100 liters) of wine annually. The yearly output varied depending on not only temperature, precipitation, and natural hazards (e.g., hail or frost), but also the quality measures of the vintners. Though historically ranked at the bottom of the list of the twenty leading grapevine countries by vineyard area, in the late 1990s and early 2000s, Germany climbed to number ten with respect to the volume produced due to higher productivity. Designated areas in thirteen wine regions restricted vine planting with regional yield limitations. These regions differed not only in size but also in varietals, wine styles, production methods, and organization.

Half of the wineries in Germany exited production in the 30 years from 1989 until 2019. While the number of producers decreased, total vineyard area remained constant. More than 7,000 entrepreneurial entities were engaged as independent producers. These estates were predominantly family-owned businesses, with a business model to produce and sell branded wine and spanned the value chain from planting, growing, harvesting, and production, to sales and marketing. Most owners followed the footsteps of their ancestors in taking over the wine-growing estate. In a market with many domestic and imported players, wine producers needed to position themselves in the market. The majority of German vintners were positioned on wine quality and price-value-proposition, but 15% of German wine estates pursued a premium strategy (**Exhibit 5** presents an overview of the generic strategies in the German wine market).[4] The market, however, provided opportunities for value creation. One was the presence of new market entrants that pointed out opportunities for profit and attractiveness. A second was that studies illustrated that the performance of the wine estates depended on innovativeness as well as the ambition level of the owners.[5] Several wine estates reported continuous annual growth and augmented their market share.

Wine was produced by vertically integrated players who owned vineyards, by de-integrated players who sourced grapes from the market, or in the case of a cooperative, individual ownership of vineyards and joint production and marketing. The downstream part of the industry consisted of direct and indirect selling channels (see **Exhibit 6** for the wine industry value chain).

WEHRHEIM'S ORIGIN STORY

Located in the central southwest of Germany, the Palatinate region shared a border with France. In 1921, in the town of Birkweiler, Karl Wehrheim started a wholesale enterprise selling agricultural products. During the Depression (1929-1941), his customers often lacked the cash to pay for the products and bartered farmland instead. Karl planted vines on the acquired land and gradually transitioned from agricultural wholesale to wine production. When Karl handed the business over to his son, Heinz, in 1947, the vineyard area amounted to about 15 acres. While his father sold bulk wine and grapes, Heinz began producing bottled wines that he sold to customers. Heinz named the business Dr. Wehrheim Winery (from the original "Weingut Hohenburg") and sought to produce wine that reflected the soil and the microclimate ("terroir") of the region. In 1984, Heinz's son, Karl-Heinz, succeeded him and took on several initiatives to grow the winery. He formed an informal partnership with five premium wineries in the Southern Palatinate region and joined the Association of German Premium Wines (VDP)[6] in 1991, one of the first wineries to do so from the region. The VDP was a selective group of about 200 quality-oriented German vintners who were committed to restrictive production standards and joint marketing. In 2007, Karl-Heinz transformed the winery into biodynamic farming and obtained European Union certification for organic production in 2010. Biodynamic farming required the conversion of all processes to organic farming methods (such as avoiding pesticides) alongside using an astrological sowing and planting calendar.[7] His efforts at transforming his winery were recognized by an industry publication:

> Wehrheim . . . is one of those high-profile estates in the southern Pfalz (a synonym for the region). Karl-Heinz Wehrheim is very active in the VDP, does the marketing for the Pfalz, has many other activities, and he is one of the trendsetters in the southern Pfalz. When, in the eighties, the Pfalz was losing territory, the young Karl-Heinz Wehrheim was one of the initiators, together with four other estates, to work together, share experiences, and evaluate each wine to improve the quality. The result of this initiative was that soon the Pfalz producer of cheap bulk wine of low quality transformed into a wine region with many excellent wines. Wehrheim companions of the early days are the now famous vineyards such as Becker, Kessler, Rebholz, and Siegrist. Cooperation, not competition, open exchange of experience, and internal criticism has ensured the success of these companies and are a stimulus for the entire Pfalz.[8]

Karl-Heinz's son, Franz, joined the business as a fourth-generation winery manager in 2017. After graduating from high school, Franz was unsure about joining the family winery. He completed an undergraduate degree in business from the

University of Mannheim. Franz talked about his initial ambivalence in seeking a career in the family business and his subsequent change of mind:

> I must admit that I was initially not very keen on joining the family business. I felt it would restrict me and hold me back from wanting to see the world and exploring opportunities elsewhere. My 'bildungsroman'[9] moment, so to speak, happened after a long talk with my father, where I could see what the winery meant to him and his quest to uphold the family's winemaking skills. An additional motivation was that all my colleagues in business school and the successful people I met showed great admiration for wine and winemakers. I then took a very practical route before joining the family firm. I went back to college and studied winemaking and worked elsewhere before working for my dad. I was quite clear with my dad, though, in telling him that I want to make my mark in this business.

At Wehrheim, Franz was responsible for sales and distribution, while his father focused on operations. While working at his family's winery Franz completed his MBA in Wine, Sustainability, and Sales, and his master's thesis was on effectual and causal decision-making in the industry. Karl-Heinz and Franz articulated their philosophy for Wehrheim as: "a harmonious, balanced integration of traditional values and innovation allowing the winery to produce unique wines of outstanding quality."[10]

Exhibit 7 provides a timeline of key events in Wehrheim's history.

WEHRHEIM'S BUSINESS MODEL

In 2022, Wehrheim owned 18 hectares (about 50 acres) of vineyards in the Palatinate wine region. The winery produced predominantly white wines (e.g., Pinot Blanc and Riesling) but some red wines in 15% of their vineyards (e.g., Pinot Noir). Oak barrel vinification refined the soil and terroir characteristics of the wines. When Karl-Heinz planted Pinot Blanc and Pinot Gris he anticipated a shift in climate and consumer preferences:

> On the one hand, I expected a change in consumer tastes towards internationally reputed varietals. On the other hand, I recognized the impact of climate change and global warming. I gained the impression that the burgundy varietals can cope with higher temperatures and more extreme weather conditions.

To secure outstanding wine quality the winery opted for lower yields. Wehrheim targeted 40 to 50 hectoliters per hectare, half the yield that wineries serving mass-market segments harvested. Annual production of Wehrheim comprised 95,000 to 120,000 (0.75 liter) bottles.[11] Sales reflected a channel mix. Direct-to-consumers, restaurants, and specialty wine shops each contributed 30% to the revenues, and 10% of yearly production was exported to foreign countries. Direct-to-consumer sales relied on more than 2,000 private customers who visited the winery on average once a year. Franz commented on the transformational sales activities:

> Only fifteen years ago, we sold predominantly in our close neighborhood and region. As a result of our increased reputation, we won clients from all over Germany, especially by supplying renowned restaurants and well-established wine stores. It is a pleasure to find our products nowadays in exciting places in the world. I would like to engage and win new clients in the world.

Two vineyard sites (Mandelberg and Kastanienbusch) produced Wehrheim's top products, which sold at a price of between €35 and €50 per bottle. Reflecting reputation and brand value, the winery´s average price exceeded the market average of €3.75 per bottle by a price premium of more than 100%. Wehrheim's wines received prestigious national and international awards in wine competitions. Neumann, a German wine guide, talked about the quality of Wehrheim's product:

> As vintners, Franz and Karl-Heinz Wehrheim stand for wines full of character, which make the regional conditions of climate and terroir tangible in taste . . . Birkweiler in Pfalz offers unique conditions for this due to its high-quality location and extremely heterogeneous soil structures. Wehrheim's wines offer harmony and balance without being sweet. They embody fullness without appearing "fat." In order to meet these requirements, careful care of the grapes on the wine and optimal aging of the wine in the cellar is essential.[12]

In addition, the Gault Millau wine guide listed Wehrheim in the top 25 German wineries.

Wehrheim shared a mobile bottling facility with three other wineries. Such a facility involved the vendor setting up a trailer onsite with a bottling unit and hoses to pump wine from the winery's tanks into bottles of designated sizes.[13] A mobile facility negated the need for capital-intensive bottling equipment (the average cost was around €500,000)[14] and enabled better capacity utilization. The four wineries worked together to ensure that each had flexibility regarding the dates needed.

In 2018, Wehrheim built additional storage space. This was necessitated by the switch to a longer aging process for the wine and a gradual increase in production.

Employee relations at Wehrheim were dictated by Karl-Heinz's statement that " good wines necessitate good teamwork." The vineyard manager, Patrick Christ, started his career as an apprentice at the winery in 1992. Christ managed the vineyards, operated the bottling machine and other technical equipment, and supervised the apprentices working for the winery. Anette Falke joined the winery in 2007 as a part-time employee to help with event management, and in 2022 was the office manager covering sales to private customers and facilitating wine-tasting events. Many of the seasonal workers who harvested the grapes by hand continued working at the winery for decades.

Karl-Heinz had continued the tradition, established first by his father, of the family having meals jointly with the employees. According to Franz, joint meals helped address managerial issues at the winery in addition to facilitating personal exchanges. In the summer months, the group would convene at the oak wood table in the winery's historic Art Nouveau farmyard and move to the large kitchen in the winter.

THE GROWTH CONVERSATION

The question of growth came up during a lunch conversation in June 2022. The trigger was a visit earlier in the day from a Norwegian wine importer. Scandinavia represented a growth market for German wines, especially for the grape varietal Riesling. Karl-Heinz had a sip of the Riesling wine accompanying the sauerkraut and liver dumplings lunch and addressed his son:

> Franz, do you share my impression that the importer from Norway this morning did not seem to be willing to commit to a longstanding partnership? Did he order wines, or did he express an appreciation for our great wines?

Franz replied:

The Norwegian importer sees great potential to win clients for our high-quality dry wines, but his main interest was in attractive lower-end wines. He stated that basic wines pave the ground for brand recognition and serve to foster demand for high-end wines from our winery. While we don't have the managerial resources to increase our international exposure, I think we need to take his idea about lower-end wines seriously for the domestic market. I do not want to jeopardize our quality standards, but I would like to produce wines to satisfy requests for easier-to-drink wines and furthermore diversify our sales channels. Increasing our sales would allow us to grow and raise awareness in the market. Additionally, the literature on entrepreneurship tells that the higher ambition of entrepreneurs pays off in higher performance. My reading is that we need to aim for growth despite a stagnant market. Indeed, I just received an offer [for us] to buy two hectares of agricultural land. If we don´t sign, one of the competitors is happy to do so.

Franz referred to peer wineries with impressive growth rates. Whereas Wehrheim had increased their vineyards by 25% in the previous 10 years, branded colleagues such as Leitz and Molitor more than tripled their wine production and had more than100 hectares of vineyards.

Karl-Heinz replied:

Land prices in our area more than quadrupled in the last 7 years. Great and famous vineyards cost more than 2 million Euros per hectare.[15] Lease agreements do not affect that price development. It remains a challenge to turn the investments into a profitable business model since wine prices remained rather stable over the same period. In addition, getting plants and material is a challenge at the moment and there is an idle time of at least three years until the yield of new plants allows [us] to produce wine.

Christ contributed to the discussion by commenting that Wehrheim had proven able to stay ahead of the competition. Falke mentioned the change in labels just three years before. Karl-Heinz stated:

The more modern image was certainly a success. But every time we carry the wines to the cars of the clients, I recognize some of our competitors' premium wineries as well as some fancy vintners in the trunk of the client's car. I remain skeptical that growth in volume results in solid profitability.

Ulrike, Karl-Heinz´s wife, who preferred to stay in the background when it came to business discussions, triggered a further need for strategic and operational discussion:

We just built the new warehouse. Was the storage capacity on site not planned for additional wine? But where does the wine come from if we do not expand the vineyards?

Franz caught up on the argument.

You are right mum, the storage capacity allows us to grow. Look at our peer competitors like Bassermann Jordan or Dönnhoff. They produce sought-for wines from their vineyards, but additionally buy premium bulk wine or grapes and enter new markets or create new brands. The growth allowed their geographical expansion. Processing sourced grapes and eventual brand extension increased their flexibility and reduced dependency on [their] own yields.

Karl-Heinz pushed back with a specific instance in mind:

We are having a dispute in the VDP organization about whether the business model of producing wine from sourced grapes is exaggerated by some member wineries. Our customers expect outstanding quality and the handwriting of the winemaker in every bottle. That was the basis for our price premium. We risk jeopardizing our quality reputation with too much volume as well as dependency on sourcing agreements. Have you seen the customer commentaries regarding our colleague from Reichsrat von Kesselstadt, who sold wine at the retail chain Aldi Süd? The wine was advertised with a quality assessment from wine publisher Falstaff. Just a few comments, but some devastating ones also reflect negatively on all VDP wineries. (**Exhibit 8** provides the customer comments).

While agreeing to drop the purchase of additional land, due to capital constraints, Franz pushed hard for his sourcing idea. He proposed sourcing grapes to create a second brand, for sales to traditional grocery chains such as Edeka (Germany's largest retailer with 11,115 retail stores across various formats)[16] and Rewe (Germany's second largest retailer with 6,000 stores).[17] These national chains carried an extensive range of wines and often used them as promotional items to attract customers. Franz argued that peer family wineries had profited from exploiting investments into production and sales to raise awareness in the market. According to Franz, their new facilities gained recognition in the local press, in the wine community, and their recognition as benchmarks in wine and tourism circles. Selected wineries were celebrated for conquering new markets and entering high-end restaurants, not only by selling their premium products, but also by leveraging this to sell a large quantity of wine in retail chains.

Even after listening to Franz's articulation of the benefits of a second brand, Karl-Heinz remained reluctant:

We risk serving as [a] short-term substitution of other brands in intermediaries' need to offer variety and permanent storytelling. The admired restaurants ask for immense discounts that meet the level of retailers with up to a 40% price reduction. Furthermore, outstanding biodynamically grown grapes are expensive. We have experienced years of scarcity in the supply of biological grapes where demand was not met. There was no market trade. How do we meet the retail contracts in years when we face lower than average yields?

To this, Franz responded:

Even expensive sourcing of very good grapes for later production in our winery does not exceed three Euros per liter. Such a strategy should not be an on-and-off decision. I envision longstanding partnerships with producers. We need to motivate the suppliers to produce outstanding quality that they sell exclusively to our winery.

While Karl-Heinz ruled out the Norwegian import offer and the idea of acquiring additional land to increase grape production, he was willing to consider the grape-sourcing idea for a secondary line of wines if Franz was able to offer a compelling argument. Putting the ball in Franz's court, Karl-Heinz pointed out that while the winery was profitable, the investments into the new storage facility adversely impacted both the profit and loss statement and the winery's cash reserves (**Exhibit 9** provides the profit & loss account for multiple years).. He added:

> New activities require adequate revenues to safeguard profitability. But pure price increases to push profitability bear risks as well. The loyal customer base is not price-insensitive, and the winery has no interest in a loss of customers. Additionally, increasing prices seems unavoidable to compensate for inflation and a dramatic surge in the cost of supply (e.g., glass for packing, fuel for tractors, etc.), far from a positive effect on profit. I heard that the benchmark winery Christmann of the VDP president Steffen Christmann announced a drastic strategic shift to lift the level of wine estate prices. The announcement stated that Christmann Winery was refraining from selling basic wines to market premium cru-based terroir wines only. This is the opposite of what you seem to favor."

Intending to end the lunch break but to keep the growth option open, Franz said:

> Dad, we should jointly agree on ambitions and vision. I see value in growth. You see growth as adversely affecting quality, a point that I disagree with. Even in the current challenging times with market turmoil because of Covid-19 I strongly recommend growing in size. I would like to seize the opportunity, that retail eagerly wants, to market premium wineries. Let us arrange sourcing agreements for grapes that serve to create a secondary brand line. We could sign a long-term purchase agreement for grapes that I was offered by a vintner friend from the university.

> Later that day, Franz shared the details of the proposal. The vintner proposed a 10-year contract for 30,000 liters of biologically grown Riesling grapes annually at a price premium of 100% to spot market terms (**Exhibit 10** shows the cost structure for Wehrheim's current production and the proposed venture). Franz felt that this proposal gave room to impose special quality requirements to not jeopardize Wehrheim's high-quality image. He pointed out that peer estates sold secondary branded wines via specialty retail for up to €6-€10 per 0.75-liter bottle and that such an arrangement, therefore, enabled a positive profit contribution. Both father and son agreed on the fact that, while no additional capital investment was needed (the increased storage capacity would be able to accommodate the additional production and the bottling cost would be a marginal cost given that Wehrheim shared the mobile bottling facility), their bank would be willing to increase their credit line to accommodate the additional working capital required. Karl-Heinz reminded Franz that he would have four weeks to make a recommendation at the annual strategy retreat.

LOOKING FORWARD TO THE STRATEGY RETREAT

Franz wanted to analyze whether growth was necessary to safeguard Wehrheim´s future by conquering new channel partners in Germany with a young and modern "Wehrheim junior offering." The yearly strategy retreat of father and son that was planned for in just four weeks seemed a promising venue to present possible scenarios and implications. Franz wondered what he should propose.

Exhibit 1 - Wine Consumption – Selected Countries

	1990	2000	2010	2016	2017	2018	2019	Change 1990-2019	Change 2018-2019
USA	20.9	21.2	27.6	31.3	31.5	32.4	33.0	57.9	1.9
France	44.0	34.5	29.3	27.1	27.0	26.7	26.5	-39.8	-0.7
Italy	34.6	30.8	24.6	22.4	22.6	22.4	22.6	-34.7	0.9
Germany	**	20.2	20.2	20.2	19.7	20.0	20.4	**	2.0
China	**	10.7	15.2	19.2	19.3	18.4	17.8	**	-3.3
The UK	7.3	9.7	12.9	12.9	13.1	12.9	13.0	78.1	0.8
Russia	**	4.7	12.2	10.1	10.4	9.9	10.0	**	1.0
Spain	16.2	14.0	10.9	9.9	10.5	10.9	11.1	-31.5	1.8
Argentina	16.9	12.5	9.8	9.4	8.9	8.4	8.5	-49.7	1.2

Note: consumption is in millions of hectoliters (1 hectoliter = 100 liters); change is in %

Source: DWI 2021, Deutscher Wein Statistik 2020/2021. Mainz, pp. 1-40.

Exhibit 2 - Wine Sales in Germany by Market Channel

	1998	2008	2020
DTC	25%	18%	10%
Special wine retail	7%	8%	7%
Supermarkets	26%	27%	30%
Discount	38%	44%	49%
Others	4%	4%	4%

Source: DWI 2011, Deutscher Wein Statistik. Mainz, pp. 1-40 and DWI 2021, Deutscher Wein Statistik 2020/2021. Mainz, pp. 1-40.

Exhibit 3 - Price of Bottle of Wine (Mid-Range) by Countries

Country	Prices in US$
Singapore	21.98
Norway	16.78
USA	12.00
UK	9.27
France	7.91
Germany	5.65
Argentina	3.00

Source: Numbeo 2022, https://www.numbeo.com

Exhibit 4 - Map of Germany's Wine-Producing Regions

Source: https://vineyards.com/wine-map/germany

Exhibit 5 - Competitive Landscape of German Wine Estates

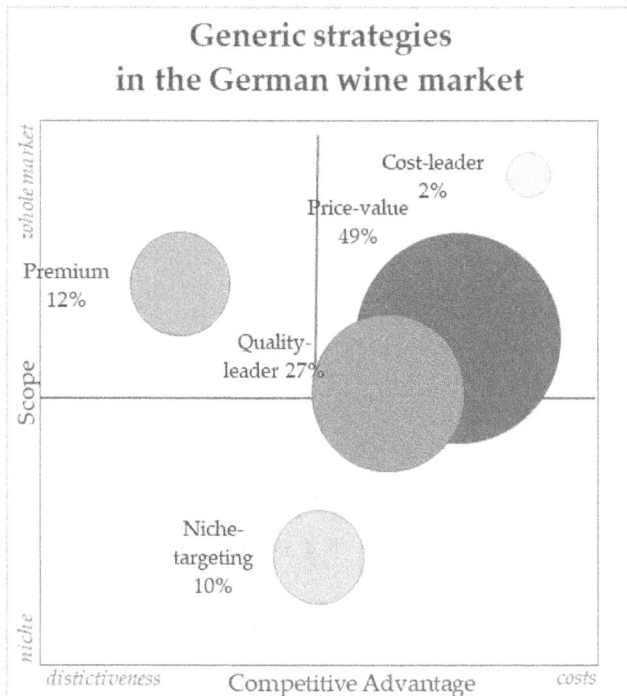

Generic strategies in the German wine market

Cost-leader 2%
Price-value 49%
Premium 12%
Quality-leader 27%
Niche-targeting 10%

whole market / *niche* — Scope (vertical axis)
distictiveness / *costs* — Competitive Advantage (horizontal axis)

Note: Per Frank T. Rothaermel (who uses the work of Michael R. Porter), there are two basic questions that a firm has to address in formulating its strategy to compete in a specific industry – scope of competition (where to compete) and source of competitive advantage (how to compete). Based on the response to these questions, the two fundamental generic (because they are context-agnostic) strategies are differentiation (referred to as "premium" in the figure above) and cost leadership. A differentiation strategy "seeks to create higher value for customers than the value that competitors create." On the other hand, cost leaders "seek to create the same or similar value for customers by delivering products/services at a lower cost than competitors, enabling the firm to offer lower prices to its customers." Instead of addressing the entire market, firms can choose to compete as differentiators or cost leaders in a specific part (or niche) of the market. Source: Frank T. Rothaermel, <u>Strategic Management</u>, 6th edition, 2024, New York: McGraw-Hill, chapter 6, "Business Strategy: Differentiation, Cost Leadership, and Blue Oceans," pp. 212-213.

Source: Marc Dressler 2018, The German wine market: a comprehensive strategic and economic analysis, Beverages, 4(4), 92.

Exhibit 6 - German Wine Industry Value Chain

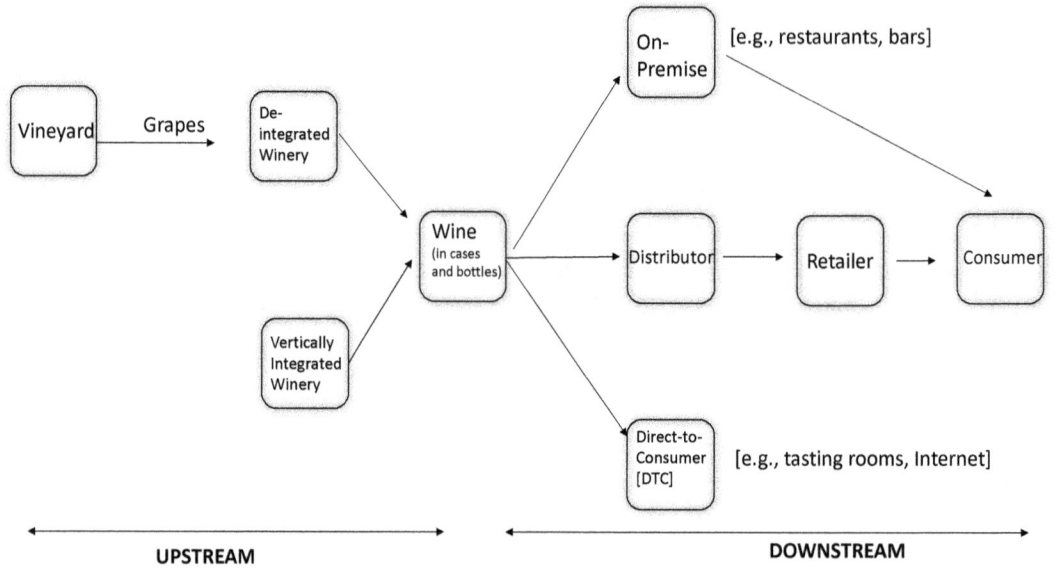

Source: Adapted by the authors from Benjamin C. Esty and Greg Saldutte, "Sandlands Vineyards," Harvard Business Publishing, Feb 8, 2018, 718438-PDF-ENG

Exhibit 7 - Dr. Wehrheim Winery Key Events Timeline

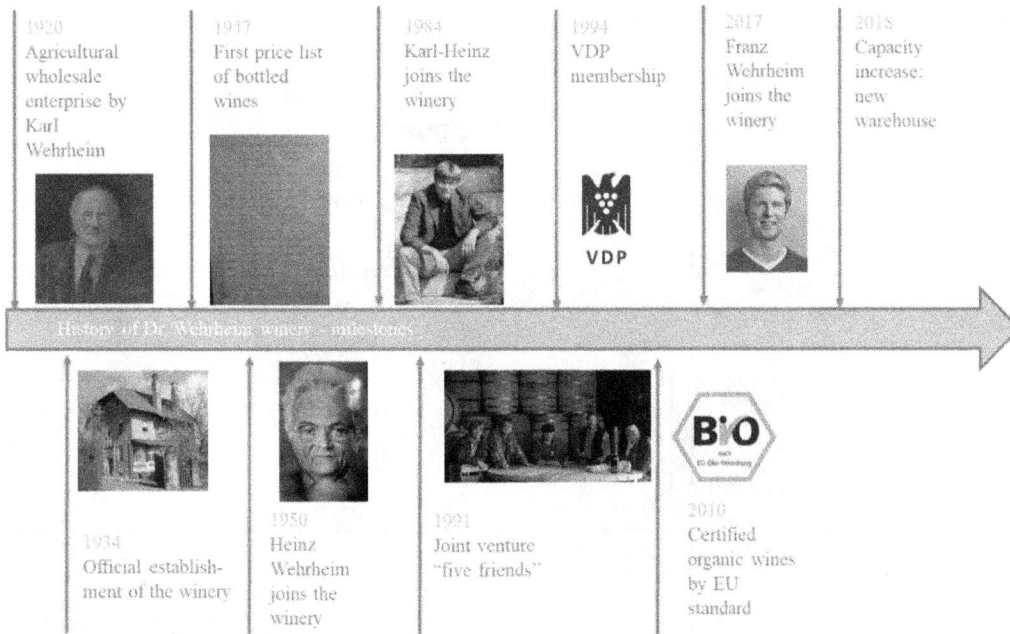

1920	1947	1984	1994	2017	2018
Agricultural wholesale enterprise by Karl Wehrheim	First price list of bottled wines	Karl-Heinz joins the winery	VDP membership	Franz Wehrheim joins the winery	Capacity increase: new warehouse

History of Dr. Wehrheim winery - milestones

1934	1950	1991	2010
Official establishment of the winery	Heinz Wehrheim joins the winery	Joint venture "five friends"	Certified organic wines by EU standard

Source: Wehrheim

Exhibit 8 - Customer Comments[18] on VDP Winery Reichsrat von Kesselstadt at Retail Chain Aldi Süd
(Product: 2020 Dry Mosel Riesling)

Rater Profile	Star Rating	Comments
Male; age 55-64	2 out of 5	**Very disappointing** I cannot understand the positive feedback. This wine – although VDP – is of lowest quality of the winery and therefore without character. You will neither find it on the winery's website nor elsewhere in the internet. Almost no flavor or taste, if at all, one can sense rotten apples. Can it be that "what cannot be sold is marketed via Aldi?"
N/A	5 out of 5	**Real deal!** Pale yellow, green-yellow color. Flavors dominated by peach; in the mouth you recognize the mosel-type acidity *[Riesling from Germany's Mosel Valley were considered to be of exceptional quality]*. Mineral note.
Male; age 35-44	1 out of 5	**VDP disappointment** A real shame to circulate such a wine as a VDP winery. Does not taste anything at all. Meanwhile the VDP quality label decays more and more. There are a lot of wineries in Germany without VDP membership producing better quality.
Female; 65 or older	5 out of 5	A wonderful Mosel Riesling, dry and very expressive
N/A	1 out of 5	**Tastes like spirit** I have really been glad to get a Mosel-wine with VDP label at Aldi. Got 3 bottles. Unfortunately, the wine tastes like spirit and is not drinkable to my taste.

Source: Aldi Süd 2022, https://www.aldi-sued.de/de/p.-riesling-vdp--l.490000000000712015.html; accessed July 28, 2022

Exhibit 9 - Wehrheim Profit & Loss Statement
(in €)

		2017	2018	2019	2020
Revenues					
	Direct to customers	304,821.00	302,467.00	305,604.00	316,822.00
	Special retail	240,162.00	252,170.00	264,779.00	327,042.00
	Restaurants	332,532.00	337,843.00	338,925.00	282,073.00
	Export	46,185.00	52,730.00	76,512.00	96,068.00
Total revenues		**923,700.00**	**945,210.00**	**985,819.00**	**1,022,005.00**
Costs					
	HR/Labor	554,220.00	565,304.00	573,784.00	592,145.00
	Supply (inc. grapes)	184,740.00	221,688.00	232,772.00	267,688.00
	Marketing	38,795.00	46,554.00	52,141.00	58,398.00
	Others	23,257.00	23,583.00	24,054.00	24,271.00
Total cost of goods		**801,012.00**	**857,129.00**	**882,752.00**	**942,502.00**
EBID		**122,688.00**	**88,081.00**	**103,067.00**	**79,503.00**

Note 1: 1 Euro equals about 1 US$ on July 22
Note 2: While the numbers are disguised, the relationship among the numbers corresponds with the original data.

Source: Authors' estimates, validated by Wehrheim

Exhibit 10 - Premium Winery Cost Structure
(in €)

	From Own grapes	Market sourced grapes
Grape Production	2.10	3.00
Pressing and Vinification	0.90	0.90
Bottling and Equipment	1.56	1.56
Distribution	2.00	2.00
TOTAL	6.56	7.46

Source: Matthias Mend, "Rechnen sich groß Weine," 2014

NOTES

[1] While last names are used to refer to people throughout the case narrative, an exception is made in the case of the Wehrheim family members. They are identified by their first names.

[2] German Wine Importers and Import Trends 2020," December 10, 2020, https://www.bestwineimporters.com/germany/german-wine-importers-and-wine-import-trends-2020/, accessed May 17, 2023.

3 While there were over 10,000 wine grape varieties in the world, Riesling was a white wine grape, native to Germany and Pinot Noir was a red wine grape that originated in Burgundy, France.

4 Marc Dressler, "Strategic Grouping in a Fragmented Market: SMEs' Strive For Legitimacy", International Journal of Entrepreneurship and Small Business, 2017, 32, 1-2, 229-253.

5 Marc Dressler, "The Entrepreneurship Powerhouse of Ambition and Innovation: Exploring German Wineries. International Journal of Entrepreneurship and Small Business, 2020, 41 (3), 397-430.

6 The acronym came from the German term for the Association, Verein Deutscher Prädikatsweingüter or VDP.

7 Carl F. Jordan, An Ecosystem Approach to Sustainable Agriculture, p. 126, Springer, 2013.

8 Westerhof 2012, https://www.bestwineroutes.com/winery/weingut-dr-wehrheim

9 A composite of two German words bildung and roman which means growing up or coming of age

10 Wehrheim 2022, https://weingut-wehrheim.de

11 Case size count varies between North America and Europe. In North America, a case consists of 12 0.75 liter bottles; in Europe it is typically 6 0.75 bottles per case

12 Neumanns 2021, https://neumanns-weine.de/product-category/winzer/dr-wehrheim

13 Alyssa Ochs, "Choosing a Mobile Bottler For Your Winery: Questions to Ask Before Hiring One," July 22, 2019, The Grapevine Magazine, https://thegrapevinemagazine.net/2019/07/choosing-a-mobile-bottler-for-your-winery-questions-to-ask-before-hiring-one/#:~:text=Mobile%20bottling%20typically%20involves%20a,the%20mobile%20bottler's%20filling%20tanks., accessed February 9, 2023.

14 http://www.thebottlemeister.com/bottling-services/full-service-mobile-bottling.php#:~:text=Bottling%20lines%20cost%20a%20minimum,equipment%20to%20maintain%20quality%20control., accessed February 9, 2023.

15 Immowelt 2022, https://www.immowelt.de/weingut-kaufen.; accessed July 28, 2022

16 Dun & Bradstreet Business Directory, https://www.dnb.com/business-directory/company-profiles.edeka_zentrale_stiftung__co_kg.f2972f0c6f5906aad8af098f7e869d16.html, accessed February 27, 2023.

17 Rewe Group, https://www.rewe-group.com/de/unternehmen/struktur-und-vertriebslinien/, accessed February 27, 2023.

18 Produced verbatim